PROSPECTS AND STRATEGIES FOR NUCLEAR POWER

Research by the Energy and Environmental Programme is supported by generous contributions of finance and professional advice from the following organizations:

AEA Technology · Amerada Hess · Arthur D Little
Ashland Oil · British Coal · British Nuclear Fuels
British Petroleum · European Commission
Department of Trade and Industry · Eastern Electricity
Enterprise Oil · ENRON Europe · Exxon · LASMO
Mobil · National Grid · National Power · Nuclear Electric
Overseas Development Administration · PowerGen
Saudi Aramco · Shell · Statoil · Texaco · Total
Tokyo Electric Power Company

PROSPECTS AND STRATEGIES FOR NUCLEAR POWER

GLOBAL BOON OR DANGEROUS DIVERSION?

PETER BECK

THE ROYAL INSTITUTE OF
INTERNATIONAL AFFAIRS
Energy and Environmental Programme

EARTHSCAN

Earthscan Publications Ltd, London

First published in Great Britain in 1994 by
Earthscan Publications Ltd, 120 Pentonville Road, London N1 9JN and
Royal Institute of International Affairs, 10 St James's Square, London SW1Y 4LE

Distributed in North America by
The Brookings Institution, 1775 Massachusetts Avenue NW,
Washington DC 20036-2188

A catalogue record for this book is available from the British Library.

ISBN 1 85383 217 0

Earthscan Publications Limited is an editorially independent subsidiary of Kogan
Page Limited and publishes in association with the International Institute of
Environment and Development and the World Wide Fund for Nature.

Printed and bound by Biddles Limited, Guildford and King's Lynn
Cover by Elaine Marriott

Contents

Contents

Boxes

To Helen, who still awaits the time when retirement will mean retirement.

Acknowledgements

So many people have assisted in bringing this study to completion, that to mention all their names would more than fill this page. They have provided comments in writing, suggested or sent sources of information, and were willing to spend time to teach an oilman some of the facts (or, as their opponents would call it, prejudices) of the nuclear and anti-nuclear life. Although it was quite impossible to make use of all the information proffered, I found most of it extremely useful in giving me a wide range of views and in strengthening my belief that both sides of the pro- and anti-nuclear divide feel passionately about their cause, and neither view should be dismissed lightly.

I am particularly grateful to Professor Wolf Häfele who, from the 1970s onwards, argued that today's nuclear technology, though acceptable when used in only a few highly industrialised countries, may not be appropriate if nuclear energy is to become a major world energy source. Without his encouragement and advice, this project would never have been started. Others, who must have spent a great deal of time looking at my drafts, made especially valuable comments. These include David Fischer, Ian Smart, Tokio Kanoh, Steve Thomas, Derek May and his staff, Simon Roberts, Ian Glendenning, Ken Wigley, Victor Gillinsky and Walt Patterson; at various points they added insights and put me right on the many errors in my drafts. In the end, however, the views expressed (as well as any remaining errors) are mine, and I take full responsibility for them.

Lastly, my gratitude is due to the staff of the Energy and Environmental Programme. I would like to thank Matthew Tickle for the effective manner in which he administered the project, together with Nicole Dando, for cheerfully and efficiently coping with all demands I made on their time. Michael Grubb, the Programme Head, has been an invaluable source of advice and encouragement. It was a pleasure to be associated with such a team.

April 1994   Peter Beck

Preface

It was in his capacity as an adviser on the Steering Committee of the Energy and Environmental Programme that Peter Beck first suggested that the Programme should conduct a study to take a fresh look at the strategic issues associated with nuclear power. We approached the subject with some foreboding: aware that almost any new contribution was likely to upset more people than it pleased; and recognising that a first problem was finding an author with extensive experience of the energy field who could take an objective and knowledgeable look at the subject, and wanted to do so, uncluttered by vested interest or a track record of being on one side or the other.

After two years without finding such an author, Peter had been sufficiently drawn into the discussions that he eventually succumbed to our persistent suggestions that he himself undertake the study. With a background in scenario planning at Shell; as a former Chairman of the Strategic Planning society; and as someone who had been thinking about the role of nuclear power for several years without being clearly identified with either 'camp', he was eminently qualified. Indeed, the fact that we were completely unable to guess his likely conclusions made him an ideal candidate.

Somewhat naively, I had wondered if the nuclear issue had lost much of its political potency after the ferocious confrontations of the 1970s and 1980s. We soon learned otherwise. I cannot recall any project on which we were under such pressure to admit more people to the review meeting, or subsequently received more unsolicited (and solicited) comments. The civility of the discussions at the study group did not hide the strength of irreconcilably opposed viewpoints and disputes even on apparently basic matters of fact. Peter received several feet of comments from every conceivable angle.

It is a tribute to Peter's tenacity that he sought to address the criticisms raised without allowing himself to be diverted from his central purpose of writing a careful appraisal of the problems and prospects for nuclear power, its potential role in future energy systems, and the strategies that might be adopted towards it. Our hosting in January 1994 of a NATO-sponsored technical workshop on the plutonium issue also enabled Peter to observe and draw on the most recent technical debates in this area.

The report reaches conclusions that will challenge many established positions: that nuclear power should be kept alive as an option to become a major global resource, but that present nuclear technologies are inappropriate for such a role; and that the future of nuclear energy is bleak unless governments act to support it, with development of a new technological path involving lower safety, proliferation, waste and decommissioning problems. Taken together, such conclusions may upset almost everyone with an interest in the issue. The project's purpose was to inspire new thinking about strategies towards nuclear power, and perhaps there will be no better measure of Peter's success in achieving this.

April 1994   Dr Michael Grubb
Head, Energy and Environmental Programme

Executive Summary

The future of nuclear energy is one of the most controversial subjects in the energy field and has become a political shuttlecock in many countries. This study examines the global prospects and strategic issues for nuclear power policy in the changed circumstances of the 1990s.

Need and urgency. Electricity demand in the next century is highly uncertain but rapid growth is probable, though depending largely on economic progress in the developing world. High energy costs and/or competition for scarce energy resources could hamper development and lead to international discord or worse. Possible climate change, not yet generally accepted as a serious threat, exacerbates uncertainty. World resources of fossil fuels could meet even rapid demand growth for many decades if concerns about global warming lessen, but not if carbon dioxide has to be constrained.

The rational response to uncertainty is flexibility. This can be achieved by ensuring, in accordance with the 'precautionary principle' of the UN Convention on Climate Change, that both nuclear energy and various renewable energy sources are options to become major energy sources during the next 50 years. The choice whether large-scale use of one, both or neither is required to balance the future energy system cannot be taken for some time. For the present, though there is no certainty that nuclear energy *must* play a major role, it *should* be maintained (or developed) as an option for strong worldwide expansion. To make a large global contribution, nuclear reactors and other nuclear facilities would have to be deployed in a wide variety of countries and conditions.

The concerns. Present industry thinking assumes that major expansion would, in addition to many more thermal reactors, involve fast breeder reactors, the recycling of plutonium via the reprocessing of spent fuel and ultimate secure disposal of all nuclear waste. However, the industry has not sufficiently resolved three important concerns arising from such a cycle, all of which have a large political content: ensuring adequate security against accidental radioactive releases; secure final disposal of long lived nuclear waste; and ensuring that expansion of nuclear energy will not increase the risk of proliferation of nuclear weapons or of nuclear terrorism.

The industry's safety record in most countries has been good, but public mistrust has forced the use of more complex and costly plant which may not be appropriate for large-scale use especially in some developing countries where high electricity demand growth is likely. Such distrust has also delayed provision for permanent waste disposal, so that such facilities are unlikely to be operational for at least two decades.

The separation of plutonium through reprocessing of spent nuclear fuel presents perhaps the most difficult area of concern. The original rationale – that it will be needed as a fuel as uranium reserves are used up – will not be relevant for many decades even with strong nuclear expansion. Reprocessing nevertheless seems likely to expand. Separated plutonium cannot at present be rendered unusable for nuclear explosives; trade and stockpiling of separated plutonium, whether pure or in the form of mixed oxide fuel, thus may increase the risks of proliferation or nuclear terrorism. Strong international supervision of stocks and movement by the IAEA may effectively prevent such dangers for limited movements between a few locations, but not if there is extensive trade between many different sites and countries.

All these factors mean that global expansion based on current nuclear technology would involve substantial – and probably politically unacceptable – risks.

Commercial factors. Nuclear power to date has prospered primarily in conditions where vertically integrated monopolistic utilities pursue the nuclear route with backing from strong central authorities. Governments in many countries are now seeking to inject greater competition into electricity generation. In these conditions gas-fired power stations, in areas with access to natural gas, usually provide the cheapest generating option for new plant, and other fossil fuel stations are more or less competitive with nuclear power depending on the required return on investment. The higher return required by the private sector makes nuclear power less competitive because of its higher capital costs. In addition, public mistrust increases lead times and unresolved issues of waste disposal and plant decommissioning could lead to indeterminate future liabilities. These factors make it unlikely that a commercial company operating in a competitive market will build nuclear stations without extensive government assurances that reduce the company's risks.

The future of nuclear energy in a specific country therefore depends on the political choice by its government to support nuclear energy.

Nuclear options. Whatever the future of nuclear energy, even if complete withdrawal were to be contemplated, today's main nuclear issues – the management of waste, decommissioning and plutonium – will require resolution. Indeed, the dismantling of nuclear weapons by the US and Russia is rapidly increasing the amount of fissile material to be destroyed or rendered safe. The ageing of commercial reactors and the phase-out of many military programmes brings the question of safe management of waste and redundant plant to the fore, so making the resolution of these problems more urgent.

Until these issues are resolved, there are few realistic options for nuclear energy. Worldwide phase-out is unlikely because of the strong support for nuclear energy in some countries; bearing in mind the need for securely dismantling existing nuclear facilities and developing alternate supplies it could anyway take 50 years or more to implement. With current technology, major global expansion is too risky, and economically and politically implausible. This leaves continuation of the status quo, with some governments continuing to believe in and support nuclear energy, but others avoiding it or terminating their interest. In this case some new stations would be built but the percentage contribution to global energy supplies would decline. Such development in itself is unlikely to be a basis for later worldwide expansion, but it may provide time to develop technologies and institutions better suited to such expansion.

Technological developments during the last decade have shown new ways of improving the safety and security of nuclear fuel cycles by considerably reducing the waste problem and dangers of proliferation. There has also been progress in the design of simpler and safer thermal reactors, suited to a wider variety of countries and utility structures. However, to prove such possibilities and bring them to the stage of being commercially available would need substantial effort culminating with testing on a commercial scale. This might take 20-30 years and cost many billions of dollars. Such a delay could be acceptable and might be used to build up the international institutions likely to be needed if large scale expansion of nuclear power were to take place.

There must, however, be grave doubts whether funds for such a programme will be found under present circumstances. The private sector would find it too risky and long-term and governments are trying to cut back on such funding. Only if seen as a security matter (which it is) might government funds be forthcoming.

Next steps. Pursuing such a programme requires first a far better understanding of, and consensus about: whether the new developments could lead to a safe, economic and acceptable world-scale nuclear industry; what such an industry might look like; whether and how these or other options can resolve the existing waste and plutonium problems; and what effort is needed to get from here to there. This requires a major international study to assess and develop some consensus on these issues, perhaps akin to that of the Intergovernmental Panel on Climate Change.

Changing energy, economic and environmental circumstances, and the accumulation of problems associated with existing nuclear technologies, have brought nuclear energy policy to a crossroads. This and the end of the Cold War, the disintegration of the USSR, nuclear disarmament and the plutonium surplus similarly mark a turning point for the non-proliferation regime which is due for fundamental review and perhaps reconstruction in 1995. The institutional and substantive relationships between the two fields make the 1995 NPT Extension/Review Conference an ideal opportunity for designing and launching such an international process of assessment and consensus-building on global strategies for nuclear power.

Introduction

The future of nuclear energy is under debate in many countries. At present it supplies some 6% of the world's primary commercial energy by providing around 17% of its electricity. Some 430 reactors with a total capacity of some 330 GWe are in operation, of which 70% are in OECD countries. Demand for electric power is set to increase dramatically, possibly to double in the next 20-25 years and to rise by one-third within ten years, with much of the expansion taking place in the developing world. Taking into account the present nuclear building programme the proportion of nuclear electricity is bound to fall during that period. As some 60% of reactors may have been retired by 2020, a building programme of some 500-600 reactors over the first twenty years of the next century may well be needed merely in order to regain the 17% proportion. There are currently no signs of such a programme and only a few countries continue to be committed to the expansion of nuclear power; indeed, in some countries popular opinion has forced governments to look at ways of reducing reliance on nuclear energy, while in most developing countries the question is whether it can or should play a significant role in the future.

Unfortunately for those having to take decisions on the mix of future generating capacity – often politicians – there is violent disagreement amongst experts (or more accurately, people considering themselves experts) about most aspects of nuclear energy. For anyone proving conclusively that nuclear energy is economic, safe and essential to ensure adequate energy for the future of mankind, there is someone else who proves equally conclusively that the energy form is dangerous, quite uneconomic and an unnecessary option for the future. One way of deciding the issue is to choose one set of advisers and ignore the others, but quite often rival political parties choose different sides and the future of nuclear power becomes a political shuttlecock. Instead of the choice being based on the decision-maker's judgment and understanding of both sides of the argument, it can become no more than an exercise in tribal prejudice.

The prime purpose of this study is not to take sides in the debate, but to widen its horizon to global strategic issues, which, though vital to the future of nuclear power, tend to be ignored in the heat of the local battles. Although concentrating on the longer term, the aim of this study is to provide understanding relevant to decisions that have to be made during this decade.

Three main issues are addressed.

1   Bearing in mind the vast uncertainties of future electricity demand, especially in the developing world, plus the probable need to constrain use of fossil fuel, does the world need to retain the flexibility for nuclear energy to become a major energy resource?

2   Under what conditions could one foresee nuclear energy becoming a generally accepted major energy resource for the world? This implies, *inter alia*

   (a) acceptance by the international community that such an expansion will not increase risks of nuclear weapons proliferation and of nuclear terrorism;
   (b) that the nuclear industry finds ways of reassuring the general public, at least in most major countries, that its facilities are safe and that it has found acceptable ways for the final disposal of nuclear waste; and
   (c) that the technology of nuclear energy becomes suitable for use in many countries of the developing world.

3   The public, the industry and individual governments have usually quite different perceptions of the risks and benefits involved in making the nuclear choice. These differences are examined to assess under what circumstances nuclear energy could become a realistic choice for utilities and/or governments. In this connection, the effect of the changing structures of the electricity markets in a number of countries is also examined.

The study goes on to consider the feasibility of some alternative global developments for nuclear energy, such as major expansion using existing technology, a minor role leading to a phase-out, and continuation of today's ambiguous situation. Finally, it assesses the possible effect of the latest technologies, which are as yet undeveloped for commercial use.

The next two chapters provide the background for the subsequent analyses. Chapter 2 gives a (very simplified) description of the technology relevant to the nuclear fuel cycles and to concerns regarding proliferation. Chapter 3 provides a brief history of the development of nuclear energy from the bomb to the present day. An understanding of that history should go some way to explain why much of the public's distrust of this energy form, particularly its fear of major accidents and of proliferation, is connected with mistrust of experts and the perceived relationship between nuclear power and the nuclear bomb.

Chapter 4 provides a glimpse at future world electricity demand as a backdrop to the later discussion on choices of fuel to meet that demand. Because energy investment requires very long time-scales and development of new energy processes even longer ones, such a glimpse has to look many decades ahead. Environmental concerns and especially the greenhouse effect also need to be taken into account.

The choice of fuel for electricity generation is far from being just the result of rational economic calculations. It is a matter of individual decision-makers' perceptions of the risks/benefits involved. The many factors involved in such a judgment are discussed in Chapter 5, while Chapter 6 looks at the competitor fuels to nuclear energy, their advantages and limitations as a background to the consideration of the long-term need for nuclear energy.

Chapter 7 discusses three options for nuclear power in the light of political acceptability, especially in relation to safety and security: (a) a phase-out, either by deliberate decisions to forgo the nuclear option, or by starving the industry of new investment; (b) a major expansion, though at a realistic pace, especially for the first 20 years; or (c) continuation of the present situation of slow drift.

As there have been a number of important new technological developments over the past decade, another option is considered in Chapter 8: whether some of these new possibilities would provide a better basis for the long-term future of nuclear energy and whether a major expansion could await their commercialization. Finally, Chapter 9 presents conclusions and some thoughts about future action.

Nuclear Power Technology

Nuclear power is fundamentally different from power based on fossil fuels. In the latter, heat is generated by the chemical reaction of burning the fuel, whilst in the former the heat is produced by nuclear fission (see Box 1 for a description of this process). Because many of the issues surrounding nuclear energy relate to the technology of the various stages involved in preparing the fuel, producing power and handling the spent fuel, this chapter outlines the main steps involved in the process as a background to the later discussions.

Another factor likely to affect the future of nuclear power is its connection with the internationally difficult and controversial area of nuclear weapons proliferation and the potential threat of such weapons becoming available to terrorists. Some indication of the technology of this connection is therefore also given in this chapter.

2.1 Nuclear reactors

Nuclear reactors lie at the heart of nuclear power. They provide the conditions for maintaining a controlled nuclear chain reaction, which releases the heat to raise steam for generating electricity.

There are two basic types of nuclear reactor. One utilizes slow neutrons for the fission process and is called a *thermal reactor* because the neutrons are slowed to 'thermal' (i.e. moderate) temperatures. The other makes use of very energetic – fast – neutrons as released in the fission reaction and is termed a *fast reactor*. All commercial power reactors are of the thermal type.

(a) Thermal reactors

In addition to fuel and a coolant to remove heat from the reactor core, thermal reactors have to make use of a moderating material to reduce the speed of neutrons released in fission to the energy most suited to the fission process.

Box 1 The nuclear fission process

When atoms of certain heavy elements, such as uranium, are bombarded by neutrons (which are elementary particles at the centre of atoms) they can, by absorbing a neutron, split into atoms of lighter elements, emitting two or three new neutrons and a considerable amount of heat. This process is termed 'nuclear fission' and the elements produced are 'fission products'. If, on average, one of the new neutrons initiates further fission, a chain reaction is sustained. The purpose of nuclear power reactors is to achieve such a reaction and utilize the heat produced for the generation of electric power. If on average less than one neutron causes fission, the reaction stops, but if more than one neutron causes new fission, neutron emission increases exponentially; under the right conditions (see Box 2) this causes a nuclear explosion.

Naturally occurring uranium is largely a mixture of two uranium isotopes,* U-238 and U-235. Although both are fissionable, fission of the former requires very high-energy neutrons and cannot be utilized in today's nuclear power reactors. On the other hand, U-235, which is present in natural uranium at a concentration of around 0.7%, can be fissioned by low-energy (called 'thermal') neutrons; such a material, which is termed 'fissile', is the basic fuel for nuclear power reactors. Although U-235 is the only naturally occurring fissile material, other artificial ones can be produced by neutron bombardment of U-238 and thorium[†] (Th-232), such elements being called 'fertile'. These can capture a thermal neutron, and the capture can initiate a reaction culminating in the formation of a fissile isotope: the artificial element plutonium in the form of Pu-239 in the case of U-238; and the artificial uranium isotope U-233 in the case of thorium.

Nuclear reactors tend to have only low concentrations of fissile material in their fuel (3-5% for most commercial designs), with most of the rest consisting of the U-238 isotope. Conversion to plutonium therefore takes place in nuclear reactors; indeed that is the usual way of producing this material. Besides fissioning, Pu-239 can, when struck by a neutron, form the Pu-240 isotope, which in turn can, by capturing a further neutron, form Pu-241, etc. The longer the fuel stays in the reactor, the more such isotopes are formed. Plutonium from commercial reactors therefore contains only some 60% Pu-239, the rest being the isotopes of higher atomic weight.

A series of reactions producing a number of other elements in their various isotopic forms also takes place in a nuclear reactor. Together with neutron-absorbing fission products these elements can 'poison' the fission chain reaction by absorbing neutrons. The fuel has therefore to be removed from the reactor well before most of the fissile material has been converted. The spent fuel is highly radioactive and has therefore to be handled and stored to ensure appropriate containment. Its radioactive decay is accompanied by emission of α and β particles (see glossary) and, for some isotopes, by electromagnetic radiation (gamma rays), together with the generation of a considerable amount of heat. It is that radiation which makes such materials biologically hazardous, and therefore in need of secure containment. Although some radioactive materials have to be safely stored for many centuries or even millennia, others decay quite rapidly, so that safe containment even for a few years or decades can improve the handling characteristics of the spent fuel. Such fuel can then, if desired, be chemically reprocessed, as described later in this chapter, by removing the fission products and separating the plutonium from the residual uranium for use in the fabrication of fresh fuel.

*Many chemical elements have a number of *isotopes*, all of which have identical chemical properties, but different atomic weights.
† Thorium has so far not been used in the commercial nuclear power programme, although India may be considering such a step.

Graphite and heavy water[1] are very effective moderators, so that reactors making use of such moderators can utilize natural uranium fuel. By far the most common moderator, however, is normal 'light' water, even though water absorbs neutrons so that reactors using such a moderator require fuel in which the concentration of the fissile U-235 isotope is increased, usually from 0.7% of the natural uranium to 3-5%.

The U-235 in normal uranium fuel can be substituted by plutonium derived from the reprocessing of spent fuel. Such mixed oxide (MOX) fuel is being cautiously introduced in an increasing number of countries,[2] although for technical reasons no more than one-third of the reactor fuel can be substituted unless significant modifications to the core of the reactor are made.

Although many different types of thermal reactors have been developed, one type has become predominant. Some 85% of today's reactors are light water reactors (LWRs), which use water either in liquid form – the pressurized water reactor (PWR) – or when boiling – the boiling water reactor (BWR) – to remove the heat from the reactor core.

(b) Fast reactors and fast breeder reactors
In fast reactors the fuel is a mixture of plutonium and uranium oxides and operates with 'fast' neutrons; there is no moderator to slow down the neutrons. Generally, the fuel has a fissile material content in the region of 15-30%, instead of the 3-5% of thermal reactors. The core is small and compact compared with those in thermal reactors, and because of the very high heat production this causes (and because water would act as an undesirable moderator) most fast reactors use liquid sodium, not water, to remove heat from the core. The sodium itself becomes radioactive in the process and has to pass its heat load to a second sodium circuit, which is in turn used to raise steam for power generation.

In fast breeder reactors (FBRs) the fast reactor core is surrounded by a blanket of uranium, derived from depleted uranium from enrichment plants and therefore with a low content of U-235. The fast neutrons from the nuclear reaction convert some of the U-238 in the fuel and blanket to plutonium,

---

[1] Heavy water is water in which the normal hydrogen isotope is replaced by the heavier deuterium isotope of hydrogen.
[2] Largely in France, Japan, Germany and Belgium.

and more plutonium can be produced than is used up in the fuel; hence the term 'breeder'. With such 'breeding' it becomes possible to extract far more energy from a unit of natural uranium, rather than having to depend on just the 0.7% of U-235 in natural uranium. Although FBRs were some of the earliest experimental reactors and by the early 1970s some semi-commercial prototypes which were technically successful were coming on-stream, scale-up to fully commercial units is proving more difficult and expensive than envisaged by the industry so that no full-scale demonstration unit is as yet operating satisfactorily.

Control
Control of all types of reactors is a matter of ensuring an adequate availability of neutrons for the chain reaction to be sustained on a constant basis, i.e. neither to stop (the reactor becoming 'subcritical'), nor to get out of hand (the reactor to become 'supercritical'). This regulation is achieved by inserting or removing control rods made of a material – usually boron – which is an effective neutron absorber. For reasons of safety, the reactors are encased in very strong containment structures.

2.2. The nuclear fuel cycle

Nuclear power reactors lie at the centre of a wide range of separate activities which together comprise the nuclear fuel cycle. Figure 2.1 shows a schematic diagram of the cycle as well as 'order of magnitude' indications of quantities involved in the various stages for the yearly operation of a typical 1,000 MWe reactor, such as is now in operation in many countries.[3]

The fuel cycle can usefully be classified into the *front end*, comprising those elements involved in preparing the fuel for the reactor, and the *back end*, comprising the various activities involved with the spent fuel once it has left the reactor.

(a) The 'front end' of the fuel cycle
Here operations can usefully be divided into four stages:

---

[3] Data derived from the Uranium Institute fact sheet 'Radioactive Waste and the Nuclear Fuel Cycle', London, August 1992.

Figure 2.1 The nuclear fuel cycle

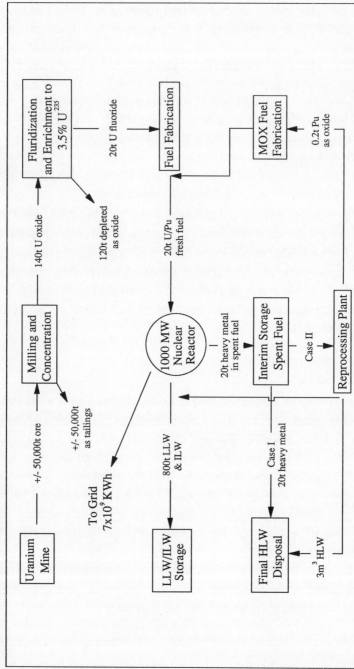

Notes: The diagram above shows the approximate yearly flows of materials for the operation of a 1,000 MW(e) LWR. Case I, no recyling. Case II, recycling.

Source: Drawn by author, based on Uranium Institute fact sheet 'Radioactive Waste and the Nuclear Fuel Cycle', London, August 1992.

1 *Mining:* Uranium ore is found in many areas of the world and in very different geological settings; its occurrence in the Earth's crust is more common than that of tin. Around half of the uranium now being produced comes from open pit workings or as a by-product of other mining operations; the other half is mined in underground mines.

2 *Milling:* The ore from the mine is treated to produce a concentrate, called yellowcake, containing some 80% uranium oxide. Depending on the quality of the ore, for each tonne of yellowcake some 500-2000 tonnes of mildly radioactive tailings are rejected.

3 *Enrichment:* As already noted, for most reactors the concentration of the U-235 isotope has to be increased above its natural level of 0.7%; the fuel has to be *enriched,* generally to a U-235 content of 3-5% for light water reactors. This is technically a demanding step, as it involves the separation of two isotopes and can therefore not be achieved by chemical means. It is normally accomplished by first converting the oxide to uranium hexafluoride and then passing that product through complex separation processes.

4 *Fuel fabrication:* Most reactors use uranium oxide, fabricated into small ceramic pellets encased in tubular zirconium alloy cladding. Some older ones use uranium metal encased in metal cans.

(b) The back end of the fuel cycle
There are two fundamentally different approaches to what happens after the fuel is removed from the reactor:

1 *Temporary storage:* The first stage is common to both. Spent fuel from nuclear reactors is initially put into temporary storage, mostly special water-filled ponds at the reactor sites, so that much of its most intense radioactivity can decay. After a few years it can be removed either to final disposal facilities for nuclear waste or to reprocessing plants.

When spent fuel from such temporary storage facilities is sent straight for permanent disposal and not re-used, the cycle is in effect open and this is generally termed the *once-through cycle.* When the spent fuel is sent from the temporary storage to reprocessing facilities and the uranium and plutonium is recovered for re-use, there is a *closed cycle* (although in practice only partially so).

2 *Reprocessing*: The prime purpose of reprocessing plants within the closed
   fuel cycle is to separate plutonium and uranium from the spent fuel so that
   these can be recycled to produce fresh fuel for nuclear reactors. In addition, reprocessing separates the radioactive waste which has accumulated
   in the spent fuel. To achieve these aims, the spent fuel is chopped up and
   dissolved in an acid bath, whereupon the different components can be
   separated. The uranium and plutonium are recovered, while the other fission products are turned into forms suitable for permanent disposal. The
   materials handled in such a plant are highly radioactive and some of the
   waste products require the highest possible level of containment. As a
   result, such plants are complex and expensive, even though the chemical
   processes involved are relatively simple. Since they rely on chemical separation, such plants can only separate different elements from each other,
   e.g. plutonium from uranium, but *cannot* separate isotopes of the same
   element, e.g. U-235 from U-238.

   In addition to military reprocessing plants in all nuclear weapons states,
   there are major civil reprocessing plants in operation in France, the UK,
   Japan and India, while Russia appears to reprocess some civil material in
   one of its military units.[4]

3 *Waste disposal*: The management and safe disposal of radioactive waste
   is the last step of the nuclear fuel cycle.[5] Wastes are classified according
   to the level, lifetime and danger of their radioactivity into *low-level, intermediate and high-level waste*. In addition there are high volumes of tailings from uranium processing which are very low in radioactivity and
   which are normally dealt with separately.

   Low-level waste (LLW), such as materials and equipment (cleaning
   materials, protective clothing and operational waste from nuclear reactors) which may have been contaminated in nuclear installations, has to
   be kept isolated whilst its radioactivity decays, i.e. for a few hundred
   years. This is done either in underground depositories or by land burial.

---

[4] D. Albright, F. Berkhout and W. Walker, *World Inventory of Plutonium and Highly Enriched Uranium, 1992*, SIPRI/Oxford University Press, 1993. Table 6.2. provides a list of
the world's reprocessing plants.
[5] *The Management of Radioactive Waste*, A Report by an International Group of Experts,
August 1991, published by the Uranium Institute, London, provides a general review of the
subject and of practices in a number of individual countries.

Although the technology of such disposal is relatively well understood, the choice of sites involves major ethical and social considerations so that decisions on new sites in democratically governed countries have been more and more difficult to reach.[6]

Intermediate-level waste (ILW) arises largely from reprocessing operations; in future some may also come from the dismantling of redundant nuclear reactors. The policies for handling such waste differ from country to country according to the nature of the waste. Where well secured LLW repositories are available, some ILW may be disposed of in these. On the other hand, some of the more seriously contaminated ILW, such as the cladding from fuel elements, will have to be disposed of together with high-level waste.

In a once-through cycle, high-level waste (HLW) is contained in the spent nuclear fuel. Such waste is highly radioactive and will have to be kept in isolation for millennia, probably in underground repositories built in areas with very stable geological conditions, well away from the possibility of ingress of water and able to absorb the high heat emission from the waste. Although there may be no insurmountable technical obstacles to overcome, there are still areas where additional research is needed. Many countries are working on this issue and are conducting long-term underground research on the subject. Given these considerations, and the political concerns about long-term safety, it is unlikely that permanent facilities will be available for two or even three decades.[7] As mentioned earlier, that can be advantageous as it allows time for some of the most

---

[6] C.W. Bullard, 'Low Level Radioactive Waste, Regaining Public Confidence', *Energy Policy*, 712, 20, August 1992, provides a review of such difficulties in the US.

[7] See Section 7 of W. Häfele, 'On the Nature of Nuclear Power and its Future', Rossendorf Research Centre, Dresden. Paper given to Global 93 Conference, Seattle, US, September 1993. To illustrate the magnitude of such a task, it is worth looking at the present effort by Sweden to manage spent nuclear fuel from its twelve power stations, due to be phased out by 2010. Even though investigative and development work has been going on for some years, a decision on final siting and designs of repositories will not be taken before the year 2000, and construction is scheduled for the 2010-2020 period. The total cost of waste management, including dismantling of reactors, is due to cost some $8.1 billion (at 1991 prices), to be spent between 1990 and 2050. See also R. Sjöblom, 'Development and Plans for the Management of Spent Nuclear Fuel in Sweden', contribution to the IAEA Advisory Group Meeting on Fuel Management, Vienna, April 1991.

intense radioactivity in the spent fuel to decay under more controlled conditions in accessible storage ponds.

Where spent fuel is reprocessed, the volume of HLW is far smaller, but the level of radioactivity is just as high. In addition, some 14 tonnes of LLW and ILW are produced per tonne of spent fuel processed.[8] The problems of safe disposal of waste therefore remain.

4 *Mixed oxide fuel fabrication*: To produce mixed oxide (MOX) fuel, plutonium oxide from reprocessing plants is mixed with uranium oxide that has low U-235 content, and fabricated into fresh fuel containing the required percentage of fissile plutonium. Although the process is very similar to normal fuel fabrication, such facilities have to be able to handle more highly radioactive materials and would have stocks of plutonium on site.

2.3 Technical aspects of the relationship between nuclear power and nuclear weapons

As will be discussed in the next chapter, concerns about the relationship between the generation of nuclear power and the manufacture and proliferation of nuclear weapons have been voiced since the start of the civil nuclear programme. This section concentrates on the technological background to this question, with Box 2 describing the principle of nuclear explosives (though excluding thermonuclear weapons).

In the light of the information in Box 2, attainment of a nuclear explosive device by a country or a terrorist organization requires means of obtaining sufficient fissile material and access to the skills to design and assemble the device. It appears that there is by now considerable information regarding the design of nuclear weapons in the public domain, which means that acquisition of sufficient fissile material remains the major stumbling-block.

When considering that problem, one has to differentiate between countries wishing to establish a reliable nuclear armoury as a threat or defence against a potential foe and a terrorist organization or a 'rogue country', which might be satisfied by having very few devices of uncertain quality.

---

[8] HMSO, *Radioactive Waste*, Vol. 1, First Report from the Environment Committee, 1985/6, Table 2 and para. 184.

Box 2 The technology of nuclear explosives

A nuclear explosive is designed to create conditions in which for a very brief period of time the fission reaction becomes highly supercritical, with the neutron population increasing a million or so times within less than a millisecond. This is accomplished by bringing together fissile material, such as U-235, U-233 or plutonium of the required purity to achieve a dense enough mass (the critical mass) for such a reaction to commence. One way of achieving this is to fire, perhaps by the use of an explosive charge, two subcritical masses of the fissile matter at each other. The amount of fissile material needed for a nuclear explosive is closely related to the critical mass, which varies with the type of fissile material and its purity. For weapons-grade U-235 of 90%+ purity, at normal density this critical mass is around 25kg. It increases as the purity is reduced by adding more U-238, until at a U-235 concentration of 20% the material is no longer classified as a nuclear explosive.[9] Pu-239 and U-233 have a critical mass of below 10kg, and although most other isotopes of plutonium are fissionable, their critical mass varies considerably. (It should be noted that by making use of neutron reflectors, it is possible to reduce – perhaps by a factor of two or more – the mass needed in a nuclear device below that of the material's critical mass.[10])

A state is likely to require weapons it can trust, which can safely be stored for some time and which have a high chance of exploding when required. Nuclear weapons, however, are very complex, have many constituent parts and require considerable skill to assemble. There can, therefore, be no certainty that a new design will work first time unless it has been tested. In the present (and hopefully future) climate against proliferation, testing could prove impossible without attracting attention and considerable international opprobrium. Countries would therefore have little choice but to stick to the most conventional design possible by making use of weapons-grade uranium and/ or plutonium. Such material is kept under the strictest of safeguards by nu-

---

[9] John Collier, 'Environmental Impact of Nuclear Power', Proceedings of a Conference of the British Nuclear Energy Society, London, 1981, pp. 263-94.
[10] J. Carson Mark, 'Explosive Properties of Reactor-grade Plutonium', *Science and Global Security*, Vol. 4, 1993, p. 111.

clear weapons states and is unlikely to be available commercially.[11] Unless a country already has access to enriching or reprocessing capacity, indigenous production of weapons-grade materials implies the development of special plant – a difficult and time-consuming exercise, not easily concealed. The availability of nuclear power reactors only is therefore but a minor factor in the capacity to achieve nuclear weapons status.

The situation for terrorists may well be rather different. If their interest is served by having just one or two devices, and even if failure of the first to explode may provide them with the type of publicity they desire, then they can take the risk of making use of any fissile material they can get hold of. In the future, once recycling of plutonium from reprocessed spent fuel from reactors becomes more common, such reactor-grade plutonium could well become available. It will enter the international trade and there might be scope for the illegal acquisition of a few tens of kilos, especially by a 'rogue' state with nuclear power facilities and which has links with terrorists. There is no doubt that such plutonium can be utilized in a nuclear weapon, even though the design and assembly may be more difficult than when using weapons-grade plutonium.[12]

So far, no satisfactory ways have emerged of 'denaturing' reactor-grade plutonium. Dilution with other material, such as U-238 (as is done when preparing MOX fuel) is only a minor obstacle, as the plutonium can be retrieved by relatively simple chemical means; for small quantities this could well be achieved in a backyard laboratory. That is not the case for plutonium in spent fuel, which is safeguarded by the high radioactivity of the spent fuel, which requires the full panoply of reprocessing for extraction to a form usable in a weapon.

From the technical standpoint, therefore, the most important connection between proliferation and nuclear power is the potential for the misuse of reactor-grade plutonium. Under present conditions, there appears to be no solution to this problem by the available technical means alone and institutional and other political assistance will also be required.

---

[11] In the past, small quantities (a few kg) of highly enriched uranium were made available to countries for use in research reactors, but there are presently strong moves to stop this practice.

[12] Carson Mark, 'Explosive Properties of Reactor Grade Plutonium', op. cit.

It has to be mentioned that there is strong disagreement in some quarters in Western Europe about the ease with which reactor-grade plutonium could be utilized by terrorists. These sources maintain that even if a good design is available, very considerable expertise and experience would be necessary to put a workable nuclear device together. They therefore believe that the present US views greatly exaggerate the dangers of reactor-grade plutonium. Sadly, this alternative viewpoint is of little value when considering future policy, even if it is correct in practice. First, it can never be proved that it is correct, and one must sincerely hope that it will never be disproved. Second, to argue that the quality of the US experimenters, who successfully exploded a device using reactor-grade plutonium, was of a level which terrorists or states assisting terrorists would never be able to match, provides such people with a most dangerous challenge. On the basis of present information, therefore, disregarding the advice that reactor-grade plutonium in the wrong hands is a potential source for nuclear devices would be a very risky course to take.[13]

---

[13] F. Barnaby, 'The Plutonium Legacy', *Current Decisions Report 12*, Oxford Research Group Report, Oxford, 1993.

Chapter 3 19

A Brief History of Nuclear Power

3.1 A military birth

As is well known, the first large-scale application of nuclear fission was its development for military use during the Second World War in the US Manhattan Project, which culminated in the explosion of the first nuclear bomb in 1945. Because of the difficulty of amassing sufficient uranium, enriched to 90%+ U-235 (considered at that time to be essential for use in a nuclear weapon), the project also developed the route to a plutonium bomb. The plutonium was being produced from U-238 in nuclear 'piles' specially designed for that purpose. The irradiated mix from the reactor was treated to separate out the plutonium – the beginning of reprocessing technology. Its importance to the project was shown by the fact that both the first nuclear test explosion and the Nagasaki bomb made use of plutonium.

The dilemma between the potential dangers of nuclear proliferation and the possible benefits of utilizing this new source of energy for peaceful purposes was quickly recognized. To guard against the former, Senator McMahon introduced a bill to the US Congress as early as 1945 proposing to restrict the use of atomic energy to (US) national defence and to retain its secret within the US.[1] To sponsor the peaceful use of nuclear energy, the US proposed in 1946 the internationalization, via the United Nations, of all nuclear developments, for both peaceful and military use (the Acheson-Lilienthal Report).[2] Owing to the deepening rift between the US and the USSR, the plan was not adopted; instead, the US moved closer to the McMahon concept and drew a veil of total secrecy over all nuclear matters. Nevertheless, by the early 1950s there were three powers with nuclear weapons capability – the US, the USSR and the UK – which all had the three main facilities to produce weapons-

---

[1] J. Collier, 'Environmental Impact of Nuclear Power', Proceedings of a Conference of the British Nuclear Energy Society, London, 1981, pp. 263-94.
[2] A discussion is given in W.C. Patterson, *The Plutonium Business*, Paladin Books, London, 1984, Chapter 1.

grade fissile material, namely enrichment, nuclear piles and chemical reprocessing facilities. They were followed by France, which exploded a nuclear device in 1960, and China in 1964.

The first steps in utilizing nuclear energy for purposes other than weapons production were also for military use: the development in the US of reactors for submarine propulsion. After considering a number of possible reactor types, including fast reactors, the US Navy chose a compact water-cooled reactor, the precursor of today's LWR.

By the end of 1953, US policy changed with President Eisenhower's announcement of the 'Atoms for Peace' programme and the acceptance by the US of international cooperation for the development and use of nuclear energy. This involved the formation of the International Atomic Energy Agency (IAEA), which was given the dual task of promoting nuclear energy worldwide *and* preventing the spread of nuclear weapons. At the time this was felt to be a political necessity in order to 'sell' the concept of such an international agency.[3]

There was at that time great popular enthusiasm for this new technological marvel. Many countries wished to make use of it, especially as the world was then in the midst of one of its periodic alarms about future shortages of oil and gas. At the same time, however, intensification of the Cold War increased fears of nuclear war, while radioactive fall-out from weapons testing became a practical rallying point for the 'ban the bomb' movements in democratic countries which came to see anything 'nuclear' as evil. Such movements gained strength during the 1960s, the decade which saw the beginning of the environmental movement and of the belief, in a significant section of the public, that 'the expert' was not a trustworthy source of information and knowledge. Largely through the work of Rachel Carson on chlorinated pesticides and Ralph Nader on the quality of consumer products, experts began to be seen as expressing views that suited the interests of their employers or, more broadly, the 'establishment'; their advice was assumed to be biased and was therefore largely discounted. The effect of this view was – and still is – far-reaching: there is little doubt that the concerns felt, and more and more strongly expressed during the 1970s, by much of the opinion-forming public and press about the acceptability of nuclear power stem from these developments.

---

[3] Ibid, Chapter 4.

By the early 1960s, the first thermal reactors specifically built for electricity generation had started to come into operation in the US and the UK, with the USSR, France and Canada developing them some years later. The US reactors evolved from the submarine light water reactors and used slightly enriched uranium as fuel in the form of its oxide. The spent fuel in their containers could be kept in cooling ponds for many years, and very little reprocessing of civilian spent fuel was undertaken. The first types of reactors in the UK, France and the USSR, on the other hand, were more directly connected with the weapons programme and especially with the production of plutonium. They used graphite-moderated gas-cooled reactors fuelled with natural uranium in its metal form, encased in metal fuel elements which were not stable enough for long-term storage in ponds. After storage for a year or so, the spent fuel had to be reprocessed and the plutonium separated out.

Nuclear power was 'sold' to US utilities as being competitive with coal- or oil-burning power stations, and the designers and developers of the LWRs for commercial use appeared to consider perceived economics as the most important criterion. It was felt that safety could be achieved through engineering design, strong containment of the reactors and siting away from population centres.[4] During the 1960s, however, the advent of cheaper oil and the increasing size and declining capital cost (per kWh installed) of conventional power stations put pressure on the competitive position of nuclear power. To be able to continue to sell nuclear plants to utility companies on economic grounds, nuclear contractors had to achieve cost reduction by also offering larger plants. As a result, 1,000 MWe plants were being built by the end of the decade, though based on operating experience of nothing larger than 200 MWe. This meant placing less reliance on containment and siting, and concentrating safety strategy on engineering design alone. This caused serious concern to the industry's regulators, who, however, tended to be overruled in the drive to enhance the future of nuclear power.[5] The effect of this policy became clear during the next decade when these plants came into operation. They were far more complex, and therefore more difficult to operate, took

---

[4] J.G. Morone and E.J. Woodhouse, *The Demise of Nuclear Energy? Lessons for Democratic Control of Technology*, Yale University Press, New Haven, CT, 1989, Chapters 3 and 4.
[5] V. Gilinsky, 'Nuclear Safety Regulation: Lessons from US Experience', *Energy Policy*, 20, August 1992, p. 704.

longer to build, and were more costly than anticipated – thereby possibly invalidating the original reason for choosing larger plants. By that time, however, it was far too late to change.

3.2 The answer to OPEC, or even more dangerous?

Following the first 'oil shock', in the early 1970s, grave concerns about the adequacy of future energy supplies once again surfaced. The importance of secure energy supplies also became clear to all industrial countries as it was evident that even quite minor shortages could cause major disruptions and political repercussions both internationally and within countries. Energy security was perceived for the first time to be as important as military security, and nuclear energy was seen by many as the potential saviour. Assuming a 'closed cycle', with FBRs converting most U-238 to plutonium, the energy equivalent of 1 tonne of natural uranium would be some 1.5 million tonnes of oil; thus under 100 tonnes of uranium might meet one year's energy needs for France, Italy or the UK. A stock of a few thousand tonnes could therefore make most countries independent of energy crises, as long as they had all the facilities needed to generate power and to close the cycle, i.e. reprocessing plants and FBRs.

That enticing vision was further enhanced by the 'accepted wisdom' of the time that world energy demand for the rest of the century would increase rapidly and that this might well be impossible to meet unless there were a rapid expansion of nuclear power. As a result, estimates of future nuclear capacity soared, and with them the assumption that FBRs and the associated reprocessing facilities would be an essential part of the world energy scene by the turn of the century. Thus in the UK, government and industry studies estimated that nuclear capacity might have to reach between 50 and 100 GWe by the end of the 1990s,[6] and that this might include a number of commercial-scale FBRs; IAEA estimates for worldwide nuclear capacity for the year 2000 were between 1,400 GWe and 2,200 GWe.[7] Today's estimates

---

[6] Royal Commission on Environmental Pollution, *Nuclear Power and the Environment*, 6th Report, HMSO, September 1976.
[7] W. Häfele et al., 'Energy in a Finite World', Energy Systems Programme Group, International Institute for Applied Systems Analysis (IIASA), 1980, Table 9.4.

show that the UK nuclear capacity by that year may be around 12 GWe and the world's some 400. Furthermore, there are to date only prototype FBRs in operation and the UK decided in 1990 to abandon its semi-commercial prototype.

What went wrong? In the first place, the mere expectation of a large, rapid and worldwide expansion of nuclear power gave greater impetus to the anti-nuclear lobby, especially in the US. It argued that such an expansion would bring many more reactors into operation; would they be safe enough? The nuclear industry's firm assurances were rather dented, first, by a bizarre incident in 1975 when a candle started a fire in a new station at Browns Ferry which damaged most of the safety systems and made the plant inoperable; and then, more seriously, by an incident at the Three Mile Island nuclear station in 1979 which caused a partial reactor core melt-down. Both these events were of a type which the industry had maintained was most unlikely to occur, and public confidence was not helped by the suspicion (recently confirmed by some of the main players of the time)[8] that regulators had approved the designs of such plants, even though some important safety proposals had not been included.

Another argument used to great effect was to question whether many countries or indeed private industry in the US could be trusted with the operation of reprocessing plants, bearing in mind that such plants have to deal with highly dangerous radioactive by-products as well as with plutonium, with all its dangers for weapons proliferation. Such arguments proved to be effective at the political level when the US government appeared to accept the conclusions of a major study sponsored by the Ford Foundation.[9] Despite the conclusion of the Non-proliferation Treaty of 1968 and the establishment of a strong unit within the International Atomic Energy Agency (IAEA) to monitor compliance with that treaty, proliferation of nuclear weapons and their use by terrorists remained the most worrying aspect of any major worldwide expansion of nuclear power. President Ford gave voice to these concerns in 1976; this was followed by a major policy statement by President Carter in April 1977.

---

[8] 'In the Shadow of the Atom', Panorama, BBC Television, September 1993.
[9] Nuclear Energy Policy Study Group, S.M. Keeny Jr. et al., 'Nuclear Power Issues and Choices', sponsored by the Ford Foundation, Ballinger Publishing Co., 1977.

The new US nuclear energy strategy considerably strengthened safety regulations for nuclear reactors, stopped work on the US FBR programme, put major obstacles in the way of commercial reprocessing, causing the abandonment of commercial reprocessing in the US, and put severe restrictions on the export of nuclear fuel. This initiative, the increasing antagonism in many localities to nuclear facilities, plus the persistent cost overruns and ever-lengthening construction time of plants, led to disillusion and the virtual abandonment of new nuclear power projects by the US electricity industry; there have been no new orders for reactors since 1978.[10] Even though some of the restrictions on commercial reprocessing were lifted by President Reagan, there have been no takers so far. This proved just as well, because in 1993 President Clinton toughened up US policy on reprocessing yet again.[11]

Other studies, such as in IAEA and at IIASA,[12] recognized the need to improve safety and safeguards against proliferation if nuclear energy was to become acceptable as a major world energy resource. The means suggested, however, lay in the sphere of increased international cooperation and control, which, with the Cold War at its height, was not seen as practicable.

The attitude of the US administration in 1976-80 greatly strengthened the anti-nuclear movements around the world. When it came to the choice of relying heavily on energy imports or on a major contribution by nuclear energy, only France and Japan, out of all the governments in the democratic world, had the tenacity to persist with the nuclear route. Disappointing results and strong public pressure caused most of the rest to slow down or even to stop nuclear development.

Both France and Japan, as well as the UK and the USSR, continued to plan the introduction of FBRs, which required spent fuel to be reprocessed so as to stockpile plutonium for such reactors. As Japan's large-scale reprocessing facilities were then only in the initial planning stage, the country was keen to

---

[10] S. Thomas, *The Realities of Nuclear Power*, Cambridge University Press, Cambridge, 1988, Chapter 4.

[11] The White House Fact Sheet of September 1993, 'Non-proliferation and export control policy', states, *inter alia*: 'The United States does not encourage the civil use of plutonium and, accordingly, does not itself engage in plutonium reprocessing for either nuclear power or nuclear explosive purposes.'

[12] W. Häfele and C. Marchetti, 'Depositories of Irradiated Fuel Elements and Long-Range Energy Perspectives', IIASA, Austria, 1977.

have its spent fuel temporarily reprocessed elsewhere. Utilities in other countries were also interested in such 'toll reprocessing' as this would reduce local constraints on the storage of spent fuel; in the case of Germany, reprocessing contracts were part of government requirements for operating licences.[13] Because of these pressures, France and the UK decided to build major new facilities at Cap de la Hague and Sellafield respectively to reprocess for other countries in addition to treating their own spent fuel. Long-term contracts for toll reprocessing were entered into, involving high prepayments and other onerous conditions for the customers. They also had to agree to take back all the plutonium and the equivalent in radiological terms of all the nuclear waste recovered from their fuel. At the time, it was confidently expected that permanent facilities for the storage of nuclear waste (including HLW) would be in place during the 1990s, when these contracts were due to start, and that commercial FBRs would be ready to come into operation. In the event, there are today no permanent HLW repositories, no commercial FBRs and no firm plans about what to do with much of the recovered plutonium.

One strong argument against taking the nuclear route, advanced by the environmental lobby during the 1970s, was the assertion that there was no need for nuclear energy and therefore for taking all the risks associated with that choice. Instead, the world could match energy demand and supply by concentrating more on improving energy efficiency and by developing renewable energy resources, such as solar power, wind, waves, tides, biomass etc. Conventional energy analysts strongly disagreed with this view, but, for reasons mentioned earlier, the environmentalists' view attracted much public support.

These diametrically opposed certainties of the pro- and anti-nuclear camps generated passionate public debate. Although many governments remained publicly committed to the nuclear cause, their determination to force through nuclear plans against public opposition varied greatly. Unfortunately, relatively few policy-makers and commentators recognized the fundamental technical, economic and political uncertainties, and argued that sensible decisions could not be taken without first achieving a better understanding of the issues involved. One who did take this view expressed it at a Royal Institution forum on nuclear energy in 1977:

---

[13] 'World Status Report: Management of Spent Nuclear Fuel', *FT Energy Economist*, 22 November 1991, p. 16.

It should be a deliberate act of policy to ensure that by the year 2000 we are faced with a choice between genuine alternatives, so that if we then decide to expand the nuclear option we do so because it is not the only, but the best thing to do at the time.[14]

Too little was known about the real (as compared to the theoretical) potential of conservation and of renewable energy and there was quite insufficient knowledge about the problems of large-scale nuclear energy development.

3.3 The 1980s and beyond – an uncomfortable interlude

The conventional view of high energy growth and high fossil fuel prices was thoroughly disproved in the 1980s. Not only was growth far lower than had been assumed, but most of what growth there was took place in the developing world. Furthermore, instead of the foreseen shortage of fossil fuel there were surpluses, especially of oil and coal, and falling prices. Then in 1986 came Chernobyl. Even though the design and operating standards of the reactor were far below those of Western reactors, the terrible effect of the accident on the surrounding area and the fact that nuclear contamination spread well beyond the USSR and as far away as Lapland gave an added impetus to the anti-nuclear lobby.

During this time, controversy about the 'real' economic attractiveness of nuclear energy became more virulent, with the industry and many governments arguing its cost-effectiveness and opponents maintaining that inclusion of construction delays, low plant availability and such as yet unknown costs as waste disposal and decommission of redundant reactors made the energy form thoroughly uneconomic. Although the argument was never settled, at least in the UK the 'anti' lobby appeared to win, when the government found during privatization of the UK electricity industry that the financial institutions balked at buying a generating company which included nuclear facilities. An independent examination led them to believe that the risks and uncertainties about future costs were too great for them. As a result, the

---

[14] Lord Flowers FRS, then Rector of Imperial College, London. See B. Flowers, 'The Fast Reactor and the Plutonium Fuel Cycle', Paper given to a Royal Institution forum on 'Nuclear Power and the Energy Future', London, October 1977.

UK nuclear power stations are still government-owned, but the industry continues to maintain its position and argues vehemently that this outcome is specific to the type of privatization and ensuing structure of the UK electricity industry and is not a measure of the competitiveness of nuclear power.[15]

The impact of strong public opposition, the Chernobyl accident and the doubts about economic attractiveness combined to swing the tide against new nuclear investment. Major projects and R&D programmes were cancelled or slowed down, reprocessing schemes abandoned and investigations into waste repositories made more searching. In some countries, obstacles were put in the way of nuclear power production by limiting the amount of spent fuel which power stations were allowed to keep in temporary storage. Although, outside the US (where many projects were cancelled), most nuclear power plants under construction were completed, few new orders were placed in OECD countries. Only France and Japan continued with their stated policies to achieve high self-sufficiency through nuclear power.

Another quite unforeseen change was the collapse of the Soviet empire and with it the end of the Cold War. This made it possible for the West to achieve better and less politically constrained contact with the nuclear industry of Russia and all its past satellite countries. The main findings from such contact can be summarized as follows:

(a) By 1990 the Soviet Union had 45 reactors in operation and a further seven under construction.[16] One of the former and four of the latter are FBRs and it may well be that the development of this type of reactor has been taken further than in the West (though this could have been owing to neglect of either safety or economics, or both). There are three reprocessing plants dealing with military and some civilian material.

(b) Many of the safety features of Soviet nuclear facilities would be quite unacceptable in the West. Furthermore, the nuclear programme has left behind it many damaged and highly polluted areas, but there are indica-

---

[15] J. Chesshire, 'Why Nuclear Power Failed the Market Test in the UK', *Energy Policy*, 20, August 1992, p. 744.

[16] R. Imai, 'Nuclear Energy at the Crossroads', International Institute for Global Peace, Tokyo, Publication 67E, Paper given to the Oxford Energy Seminar, September 1991.

tions that the damage caused by the power programme is small when compared to that of the military (which has at times been stated to be even greater than caused by Chernobyl). The defects were not due to lack of skill, knowledge or dedication, but were a direct result of the dictatorial and bureaucratic system of decision-making in the Soviet state. The regulatory authority was insufficiently independent from the ministry in charge of operation and therefore from pressures to achieve targets. The scientists and engineers in these countries did not deliberately court accidents or pollution; they were under only one pressure: to produce results. Western organizations, on the other hand, have to balance these pressures with those of public demands for high levels of safety.

(c) Nevertheless, within the constraints of this system, the general quality of operation was good and average load and energy availability factors were higher than Western averages.

(d) The nuclear programme was deeply feared by the public, especially after Chernobyl, and as soon as the public voice started to have influence, the programme came under fire. For this reason, and because of the disintegration of the decision-making command structure, most of the construction of new plants has been halted. Even though plans have recently been announced to double nuclear capacity within 20 years, only work connected with safety improvement of plants is definitely going ahead and there is great uncertainty about the way forward.

Another result of the end of the Cold War was the various nuclear disarmament agreements reached between the US and Russia, involving the dismantling of a part of their 50,000 or so nuclear weapons stock. This will, over time, release some 1,600 tonnes or more of weapons-grade uranium and plutonium from military use; enough, if processed into LWR fuel, for some five years' operation of all current power reactors.[17] However, the process of dismantling, safeguarding the stock and finding a route to make use of it is difficult and costly, especially for Russia.[18] The rate of dismantling is sched-

---

[17] R.L. Garwin, 'Nuclear Dismantlement, Storage and Disposal', Resumé of NATO workshop, Erice, Sicily, August 1993.

[18] V. Gilinsky, 'Russian Nuclear Material Sales and Western Markets: The Prospect for Russian Weapons Plutonium', Remarks at a Seminar at the Université de Paris-Dauphine, 26 May 1993.

uled at 2,000 weapons per year in the US and Russia together, so that the task will take well over ten years.

As regards secure disposition, the uranium should not cause many problems as it can readily be blended with natural uranium so that it is lower than the 20% threshold established by the IAEA, below which secure storage is unnecessary. Such a blend can then be used in fuel fabrication for power reactors; indeed, the US has recently agreed to purchase 500 tonnes of weapons-grade uranium (though to be shipped below the threshold concentration) from Russia over the next 20 years. No such option exists for plutonium; as already mentioned in Chapter 2, it cannot readily be 'denatured', nor is there an immediate use either in Russia or the US. For the longer term, a number of options are available, but none are easy, quick or without proliferation risk, bearing in mind that less than 20kg needs to be stolen to fabricate a nuclear device. Thus storage and shipment of such a material will have to be under the strictest safeguards. This has been recognized by the US government, which has decided to allow fissile material no longer needed for the nuclear weapons programme to be inspected by the IAEA[19] (as a nuclear weapons state the US has up to now been exempt from such inspection).

To the concern about easier availability of fissile material has to be added the possibility of easier availability of nuclear weapons expertise. With the end of the nuclear weapons industry in the USSR successor countries, a number of cities sited in remote areas will lose their only *raison d'être*, and there is a real danger that nuclear experts in such places with experience in both the military and the civil fields will be keen to utilize their knowledge on behalf of anyone willing to employ them.[20] Consequently, we come to the perverse conclusion that nuclear disarmament may well increase the dangers of proliferation.

The final and, for the future of nuclear energy, perhaps the most important new development of the past ten years is the increasing worldwide concern about climate change. Just as mainstream energy analysts had come to the conclusion that there was unlikely to be an energy shortage for a long time to

---

[19] This decision was announced by President Clinton on 27 September 1993, in a speech to the UN General Assembly which also dealt with broad outlines of the proposed US policy regarding the dangers of proliferation; see also White House Fact Sheet, op. cit. (Chapter 3, note 11).

[20] R. Imai, 'The Long Shadow of Nuclear Weapons', Policy Paper 114E, International Institute for Global Peace, Tokyo, July 1993.

come, so did fears about climate change reach the political consciousness, and with them suggestions that the world may have to find means of reducing carbon dioxide emissions by reducing combustion of fossil fuel. If at the same time the demand for energy, which is still assumed to rise, is to be met, then means of energy production which do not generate greenhouse gases will have to be found. Clearly, nuclear energy fits that recipe well and the issue gave a large and (after Chernobyl) welcome fillip to nuclear lobbies everywhere. However, the renewable energy/conservation lobby is as determined as it was 20 years ago to argue that greater efforts than have so far been expended on the development of renewable energy and conservation technologies could overcome the greenhouse problem without help from nuclear power.

3.4 The lessons learnt

The following lessons can be learned from the experience so far.

(a) Forty years after the launch of the 'Atoms for Peace Programme', nuclear power has made impressive strides:

- It generates some 2,000 TWh per year, or 17% of world electricity.
- Some 500 reactors are in operation or under construction in 31 countries.
- Outside the previous communist area, the safety record of civil nuclear reactors has been very good, with no major accident involving off-site contamination or injuries so far.

(b) Perception in many quarters is quite different. People dwell on the many failures to achieve promised goals, the accidents, the perceived dangers from radiation and proliferation and the very high government R&D costs without which commercialization would not have been possible; they conclude that the effort was not worthwhile. Whether or not deserved, once a bad reputation sticks, it becomes very difficult to recover a good name. The industry faces a major unresolved problem: how to remove the suspicion of much of the press and public.

(c) The lobby opposed to nuclear energy has played an important role in ensuring adequate safety provisions for nuclear installations in the West.

The lack of such a lobby in dictatorships, such as in the USSR, may well have been one reason for far lower safety controls in such areas.

(d) What happened at Chernobyl showed that a major accident at a nuclear installation can have a far more widespread effect than accidents with any other source of power production and provides proof of the transnational nature of nuclear safety. The quality of safety in any one country has, therefore, to be the concern of the international community and not just of the country involved. Although the charter of the IAEA recognizes this, the Agency only has powers to advise, not to implement. Present international institutions do not have the 'teeth' to ensure safe operation everywhere.

(e) Progress with the back end of the fuel cycle has not been so spectacular. Present nuclear electricity production involves making about 9000t/yr of spent fuel, only a small amount of which is scheduled for reprocessing. In addition vastly more waste is produced from the various military programmes. Yet so far no permanent storage facilities for HLW are available anywhere. We thus have a rapidly growing stockpile of HLW and plutonium in temporary civilian and military storage. Whatever the future of nuclear power, the problem of final disposal has to be resolved.

(f) Perhaps the most important unresolved issue is the dilemma first recognized in the 1940s: how to ensure the right balance between the benefits of nuclear energy and the dangers of proliferation or nuclear terrorism. The problem has come near the top of the international political agenda a few times, usually through the efforts of the US, and each time some progress has been made, such as the formation and then the strengthening of the IAEA and the development of the international Non-proliferation Treaty, but these actions have by no means resolved the issue. That is seen by the differences of view between the recent policy announcements by the US, which confirmed the reservations expressed in the Ford Foundation study of 1977 about the desirability of entering the 'plutonium economy', and the view of other countries that they have a need to do so and that the dangers of proliferation are exaggerated.

(g) One final and worrying lesson is that the argument between the pro- and anti-nuclear lobbies is as fierce and unresolved as ever. Even though the concerns about climate change and the resulting need to reduce carbon dioxide emissions enhance the prospects for nuclear energy, enthusiasts for renewable energy sources continue to claim that they could take up the strain if given sufficient resources to develop and prove their technologies. They argue that the priority given by governments to nuclear developments – historically and still often today – robs them of this opportunity. We are thus left with the same opposing views we saw during the 1970s and we are in no better shape to make the informed choices proposed by Lord Flowers.

Some Thoughts on Future Electricity Requirements

Experience over many decades has shown that consensus forecasts of the world energy scene have had an abysmal record even when looking just one decade ahead. The idea of looking 30 to 50 years ahead might therefore justify the comment that 'it must be an even greater triumph of hope over experience than a third marriage'. No attempt is therefore made in this section to provide a forecast. Instead, aspects of the longer term are discussed to assist the later examination of the case for and against the use of nuclear energy. Any figures quoted about future electricity demand are no more than indications to provide a 'feel'.

Because nuclear energy is almost exclusively used for electricity generation, this chapter concentrates on the future of electricity demand. This is a simplification, because nuclear energy could in future be used as a source of high-temperature heat for chemical reactions such as the production of hydrogen, say to make synthetic liquid fuels. However, such a development is some decades away and is most unlikely to sway decisions on nuclear power made in the next few years.

When considering the future demand for electricity one is immediately confronted with the present enormous gap in the state of economic development between the OECD countries and the developing world (DW) and the great uncertainties about how quickly this gap will narrow, or whether it will at all. The gigantic difference in the rate of population increase between the two regions and the effect of that on future energy demand exacerbates the level of uncertainty. Although the phenomena are well known, their scale is such as to make it worthwhile to show their magnitude in tabular forms.

It will be seen from Table 4.1 that in the 15-year period between 1990 and 2005, the estimated growth of population within the DW will be larger than the total population of the industrialized countries in 1990. By 2020, nearly 85% of the world's population will be in the developing world and over 50%

Table 4.1 Estimates of world population growth: some examples (thousand millions)

	1990[1]	2005[2]	2020[2]	2050[3]
Industrialized world	1.26	1.37	1.4	1.4
Developing world	4.01	5.33	6.6	9.1
of which China		*1.14*	*1.35*	*1.5*
Total world	5.27	6.70	8.0	10.5

Note: Industrialized world includes OECD, eastern Europe and the former Soviet Union and the developing world all the rest.

Sources:
1 CEC DG XVII, 'A View to the Future', *Energy in Europe*, Special Issue, September 1992.
2 World Energy Commission Report, 'Energy for Tomorrow's World', WEC, September 1993, Reference Case B.
3 R. Eden, 'World Energy to 2050', *Energy Policy*, March 1993, p. 231.

in Asia, much of it in countries which have achieved high levels of economic growth during the past decade. Thus the GDP of South and East Asia (excluding Japan) grew at some 7% p.a. during the 1985-90 period, compared with 3.2% for the OECD. Of course, such growth came from a very low starting-point, but if rapid growth were to continue, the area would soon become an important economic factor and therefore a major user of electricity. That such a trend is already with us can be seen from recent reports that Asia will need an additional 125 to 160 GW electricity generating capacity during this decade, of which China is planning to install some 100 GW[1] (i.e. considerably more than today's total UK capacity of some 80 GW). Beyond the year 2000, growth of electricity demand in the DW could well be two to three times that in the industrialized countries.

As a number of Latin American countries are also becoming more successful, it is no longer fanciful to assume that sometime during the first quarter of the next century, the DW will overtake the OECD in economic activity, as

[1] F. Gray, 'Doors Opened to Foreign Investment', *The Financial Times*, London, 25 May 1993.

Figure 4.1 Total world electricity demand, 1970-2050

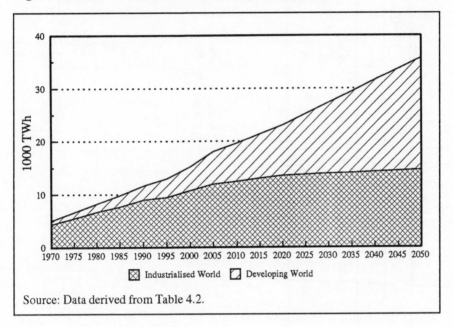

Source: Data derived from Table 4.2.

measured by GDP, and soon after that it will outstrip the industrialized countries in the amount of electricity generated. Table 4.2 and Figure 4.1 show some recent estimates of future electricity demand, which illustrate this trend.

By far the greatest uncertainty in the longer-term figures occurs in the assumption of the electricity demand per capita in the DW. This was some 0.4 MWh/yr in 1988, compared with 7.2 MWh/yr in the OECD countries. Even the high figures for 2050 in Table 4.2 only assume a DW demand per capita of 2.3 MWh/yr, a level surpassed in OECD countries during the 1960s. The reasons for not assuming higher growth in the DW are the inclusion in both the estimates for 2050 of considerable improvements in the efficiency of utilizing electricity and doubts whether generating capacity to cater for even higher growth can be funded and built in time.

There are also substantial uncertainties about demand in the industrialized world, especially regarding how far political and international pressure for energy conservation could reduce the need for electric power. Although there

Table 4.2 World electricity demand (PWh)

	1990[1]		2005[1]		2020[2]		2050[3]		2050[4]	
	PWh	%	PWh	%	PWh	%	PWh	%	PWh	%
Industrialised world	9.0	78	12.0	67	13.0	57	12.8	40	14.6	41
Developing world	2.6	22	6.0	33	10.0	43	19.6	60	21.1	59
Total world	11.6		18.0		23.0		32.4		35.7	

Note: PWh (petawatt hour) = 1,000 TWh

Sources:
1 CEC DG XVII, 'A View to the Future', *Energy in Europe*, Special Issue, September 1992.
2 World Energy Commission Report, 'Energy for Tomorrow's World', WEC, London, September 1993, Reference Case B.
3 T.B. Johansson et al., *Renewable Energy*, Island Press, Washington DC, 1993, derived from Intergovernmental Panel on Climate Change.
4 R.J. Eden, 'World Energy to 2050', *Energy Policy*, March 1993, p. 231.

is ample evidence that great improvements are possible,[2] the effect of such a possibility on total world demand is much less severe than the uncertainties concerning the DW, where the effect of efficiency improvement may not necessarily be a saving of energy, but may lead to a more rapid enhancement in the standard of living and at least temporarily to higher energy needs.[3]

Compared with 1990, the projections show that world electricity demand will double by 2020 and treble by 2050. That implies continuation of present trends in the percentage growth rate for electricity demand for the next few decades, with some slow-down thereafter. Such estimates are inevitably highly uncertain and no more is claimed for them than that they appear (at least to the author) quite credible. The data will therefore be used to consider what energy resources could meet such demand, but in doing so, the limitations of these figures have to be kept in mind; there could easily be a 30-40% margin of error for the figures for 2050, and any supply analysis has to take such large uncertainties into account.

A possible worldwide demand in 2020 of 23,000 TWh/yr would require a generating capacity of some 3,500-4,000 GW, or about twice today's total. With the exception of hydropower, most of today's plant will have reached the end of its life. We are therefore looking at as much as 3,000 GW of new capacity. Of that, around 50% would be for the developing world, implying the need for the equivalent of more than 1,500 new large stations. By mid-century, total capacity may have to be about 6,000 GW, of which perhaps 3,500 GW would be in countries now in the developing world.

How will the fuel for all these stations be chosen? This question is addressed in Chapter 5.

---

[2] See, for example, A.P. Fickett, C.W. Gellings and A.B. Lovins, 'Efficient Use of Electricity', *Scientific American*, September 1990, p. 29.
[3] H.D. Saunders, 'The Khazzoom-Brookes Postulate and Neoclassical Growth', *The Energy Journal*, 13, No. 4, 1992, p. 131.

Fuel for Electricity Generation: The Ingredients of Choice

5.1 Introduction

The present proportions of the various fuels used for electricity generation were determined by the many individual decisions of politicians, government employees and business people in all countries, each based on their beliefs at the time regarding what would be a 'good' choice. The definition of 'good' may have varied widely, from cheapness or secure supply to personal ambition, but it is safe to assume that in all cases the choice depended on someone's or some organization's judgment that the perceived benefit of the choice outweighed its perceived risk.

When looking at future choices, we have to take into account a number of radical changes which have taken place in the structure of, and demands on, the electricity industries in an increasing number of countries. Until the 1970s, most major decisions on power generation were taken by governments, or at least underwritten by them, even when, as in the US or Germany, many of the generators were in the private sector. There was close integration between the supply and distribution functions and little or no competition. Under such circumstances, risks to the public utilities were limited to technical or operational failure and even then, it was usually inconceivable that a government would let a local electricity supplier fail. Because the risk was small, a relatively small reward was accepted as reasonable by government or investor.

Since then, a number of OECD countries have taken steps to liberalize their electricity industry by breaking up monopoly structures, creating more competition, and distancing the state from major supply decisions.[1] Although most developing countries have not yet followed this path, they will undoubtedly be under pressure to do so, as lenders of external finance, such as the World Bank or various Western banks, may increasingly make such moves a precondition for loans. To complicate matters, most governments have also

---

[1] F. McGowan, *The Struggle for Power in Europe: Competition and Regulation in the EC Electricity Industry*, Energy and Environmental Programme, RIIA, London 1993.

committed themselves, in the Framework Convention on Climate Change, to an international regime which may require increasingly strict limitations of greenhouse gas emissions. Such limitations are likely to be achieved only if governments retain (either directly or indirectly, e.g. through the taxation system) a strong influence over electricity supply decisions. With many governments' energy policies apparently facing in the opposite direction and in a still untested commercial environment, assessment of the risk/benefit equation for utility companies has become far more difficult.

When considering how such risk/benefit analyses might affect future choices of fuel, the first and obvious point to be made is that assessment of future risk and benefit will always be a matter of judgment, not fact; there are no facts about the future. Final decisions will rest on beliefs about different types of risks, such as technological, environmental, safety, and political, which, when combined into overall economic judgments, are seen to stand the best chance of delivering an acceptable reward. The rest of this chapter considers the basis of such beliefs, discusses the risks facing nuclear projects and their effect on the economics of nuclear power, and finally examines how these might be affected by different structures of the electricity markets.

5.2 The formation of beliefs

When looking at individual risks, judgment will be formed, *inter alia*, by decision-makers' beliefs about what is or is not rational, by their views of a likely future and by their assessment of whether their preferred course will be publicly acceptable. (This last issue is especially important for nuclear energy, as it is generally recognized that in democratic countries there is little future for this energy form unless it is at least tolerated by public opinion.) Before discussing individual risks it is therefore of interest to examine how and why such beliefs are formed.

(a) Rationality

We all believe ourselves to be rational and tend to consider those holding different convictions to be irrational or, worse, not honest. Recent work,[2]

---

[2] P. James, P. Tayler and M. Thompson, 'Plural Rationalities', *Warwick University Papers in Management*, No. 9, May 1987.

however, has shown that we tend to have a set of convictions about the world around us that can be fundamentally at odds with the convictions of others. An example very relevant to energy, and especially nuclear energy, is our perception of nature. This varies from one stereotypical belief that nature is benign and forgiving, so that we can treat it harshly without having to worry about the consequences, to another, which considers man to be in a very unstable equilibrium with nature and that any untoward action can cause catastrophe. Most peoples' convictions fall in between, with the *laissez-faire* entrepreneur being closer to the former stereotype and the dedicated environmentalist to the latter. Worthwhile dialogue between the two extremes is difficult because neither side can see the other as fully rational and they deeply mistrust each other's motives. Hence the great lack of understanding between the pro- and anti-nuclear lobbies. Although there are many exceptions, people holding views closer to the benign model of nature tend to gravitate towards the political right and the more environmentally concerned to the centre or left, causing a divide in democratic parties' attitudes towards the environment. This can be seen in the different approaches to nuclear power by the Democrats and Republicans in the US and by different parties in Germany.[3]

(b) Forecasting

Medium-term (five years plus) forecasts of such items as demand, availability or price in the energy field have had a near 100% failure record for many decades.[4] Yet, because numerical forecasts are seen as cornerstones of much economic analysis of projects, they are still in common use. The problem of faulty forecasting is exacerbated by the fact that organizations tend to attract advisers whose beliefs are in tune with their employers' – not because of dishonesty, but because of a natural bias in the selection process, both by the employee and the employer (would someone strongly believing in the future of nuclear power ever wish to work with Greenpeace?). As a result, the saying that 'the wish is father to the thought' is too prevalent for comfort in many companies, pressure groups and governments.

---

[3] For example T. Roser, 'Germany Struggles towards Consensus', *Atom*, No. 426, p. 2. January/February 1993.

[4] P.W. Beck, 'Forecasts: Opiates for Decision Makers', Lecture to 3rd International Symposium on Forecasting, Philadelphia, 1983, Shell UK Ltd. See also 'How Shell does it in the UK', *Journal for Business Forecasting*, No. 1, Spring 1984, pp. 2-3.

To take one example, during the early 1980s the basic case for the Sizewell B nuclear power station in the UK assumed that international coal prices would rise to some $100/t by the end of this century, while in 1992 it was decided to close down much of the UK coal capacity on the assumption that world coal prices would not rise above $50/t for a very long time. Whether the decision to go ahead with Sizewell was correct or not, there can be little doubt that at the time the forecast of high coal prices received a ready welcome from a government with the political wish to reduce dependence on coal by promoting nuclear power. Because of this process of inbred forecasting, governments and companies tend to become committed to one inflexible course of action which can lead to expensive errors. Although governments are usually resilient enough to survive, it can be lethal to private companies, especially if operating under strong competitive conditions. Recently there has been wider acknowledgement of future uncertainty and this has undoubtedly increased the perception of risk when major decisions are taken in areas such as energy, where projects are large and expensive and have long lead times. Unfortunately, the result of this acknowledgement may well be avoidance of any decision – which may lead to the worst outcome of all.

The normal method of taking decisions in this area is to agree on a future against which schemes should be considered and to choose the one looking best for that future. The fact that past experience shows that the chosen future has very little probability of coming about gets ignored. Of course, once the scheme is launched and much money spent, there is little flexibility to adjust to a different future without admitting past errors of judgment, which in political terms can be the equivalent of committing suicide. Once $1 billion has been spent on a project it is far easier to make a case for the next billion than to admit failure and go back to the drawing-board. Because nuclear energy has very long lead times and high development expenses, especially when prototype demonstration is taken into account, the danger of getting 'locked in' to courses not well suited to coping with future uncertainties may well be greater than with many other technologies. Although perceptive academic work has been done on the subject of technology-related decisions made under conditions of substantial uncertainty,[5] which shows that there are

---

[5] D. Collingridge, *The Social Control of Technology*, The Open University Press, Milton Keynes, 1981; and *Technology in the Policy Process: Controlling Nuclear Power*, Frances Pinter, London, 1983.

ways of maintaining more flexibility when one deliberately accepts the reality of uncertainty, there is little evidence that much practical use has been made of it. This may be because it does not readily lead to detailed economic calculations, a *sine qua non* for the modern decision-maker.

(c) Public attitudes

In a democracy, public acceptance of, or at least lack of overt hostility towards, a large-scale project is an important ingredient for its success. Past experience with nuclear energy has shown that, without such acceptance, political and local obstruction can cause delays, heavy cost-increases and even eventual cancellation. How and why such attitudes are formed is of considerable importance, especially to the nuclear industry, which believes the negative attitude towards nuclear energy by a large section of the public to be quite unjustified.[6] Work done on this subject[7] indicates that an individual forms his attitudes for or against something by aggregating, possibly subconsciously, a number of beliefs about risks and benefits.

When it comes to the motor car, the risk of an accident and of pollution is offset by the benefit of convenience and the freedom of movement it provides and by the belief that we are in control of the degree of risk we wish to take. Therefore, the balance for most people (at least up to now) is a positive attitude towards the car, notwithstanding its risks. In the case of nuclear energy, some of the risks considered are psychological or socio-political, such as a general mistrust of large and impersonal systems, the effect of radiation on future generations, the dangers of proliferation or terrorism – all of which are vague and disturbing, especially as the risk is seen to be imposed by outsiders and thus unavoidable. An individual will not readily identify benefits to offset such risks and therefore the attitude towards nuclear energy may well be negative, unless there is strong advice from someone trusted by the individual that there is an advantage to society at large. Where the industry is seen to provide tangible benefits to a locality, such as employment,

---

[6] See, for example, P.R. Maul, W. Turner and I. Glendenning, 'Environmental Impact of Nuclear Power', *IEE Proceedings*, 13, 140, January 1993.

[7] H.J. Otway, 'Understanding Public Attitudes towards Nuclear Energy', IAEA, Vienna, paper presented to the International Conference on Nuclear Power and the Public, Geneva, September 1977. See also M. Granger Morgan, 'Risk Analysis and Management', *Scientific American*, July 1993, p. 24.

attitudes can change and there are a number of examples of this from Japan,[8] as well as from France and the UK.

Because risk perception tends to be asymmetric (i.e. worry about the consequences of a bad outcome is stronger than expectation of benefits from a good outcome), improving the chances of the good outcome, such as reducing the probability of a serious mishap from low to very low, may have only a limited effect on popular perception. For the industry this can mean that engineering solutions to safety risks may affect the views of experts rather than public opinion.

5.3 The nature of risks

When it comes to a comparative assessment of risk/benefit for different fuels, the types of risks which have to be considered are shown in Figure 5.1. Of course, the results of such comparative analysis will vary from country to country and from period to period, but the building blocks should be similar in most studies. Although all the risks are connected, understanding can be enhanced if each is first considered separately. This chapter examines technological, environmental, safety, political and economic risks; the problems of availability are considered in Chapter 6.

(a) Technological risks
These fall into two main categories. First, the technology chosen could, for one reason or another, prove unsatisfactory, say by causing delays in achieving satisfactory operation or by proving unreliable. Second, it could become outdated, with other utilities bringing in more efficient plant enabling them to gain a competitive edge. Choice of well-proven technology can reduce the first risk, but may increase the chance of the second.

Within the nuclear energy field, the LWR has become the work-horse of the industry, with third-generation designs available. Although there are a number of more novel designs on the drawing-board, past experience has shown that a utility company in a competitive environment would be unwise to choose an unproven process until the first-generation commercial plant has at least shown

---

[8] T. Kanoh, TEPCO, Japan (personal communication).

Figure 5.1 Types of risks

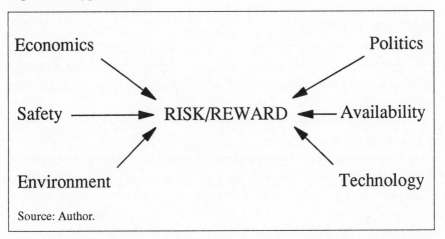

Source: Author.

the design to be sound. Bearing in mind the need for a large-scale demonstration unit before the first commercial prototype can be built and the time needed for the nuclear safety regulators to approve designs, it might well be more than 20 years before plants based on radically different designs could be safely chosen. When looking at nuclear energy in isolation, therefore, the technological risk of unreliability or obsolescence is small when choosing a well-proven reactor system like the PWR.

The situation with rival fuels, however, is quite different. The advent of large industrial gas turbines is revolutionizing the fossil fuel power generation market, especially when natural gas is used. The latest gas-fired combined cycle units (so-called because they combine power generation by gas turbines and by steam turbines) have generating efficiencies of well above 50%, compared with the 30-35% efficiency of most of today's coal- or oil-fired stations. Further developments now under consideration could increase efficiency towards 60%. As such units can be built within a year or two, such processes might already be sufficiently proven by the end of this century for commercial units to be in operation shortly thereafter. By combining the latest fuel gasification processes with the use of combined cycle technology, it is possible to gain considerable improvements in efficiency and cleanliness when using coal and even renewable 'bio-fuels', such as crops and wood. A number of prototype plants based on coal are in operation or being built and it is quite likely that commercial units using this technology will be in operation sometime during the next decade.

In summary, then, it seems unlikely that today's nuclear technology will become outdated for a number of years, but the present rapid rate of change of thermal technology will affect the relative competitive position of any new nuclear plant.

(b) Environmental risk factors
This is the area seen by many as providing nuclear energy with its greatest advantage and by many others as causing it the most difficult and intractable problems.

Advantages   The perceived advantage is due to the fact that, in contrast to thermal power generation, nuclear electricity generation does not cause pollution from flue gases containing dust, SO_2 and NOx and does not emit CO_2. When utilizing fossil fuels, the pollutants can be dramatically reduced by making use of the latest power station technology. CO_2 can only be reduced by burning fuels of lower carbon content and/or by improving the efficiency of power generation. Even with the latest coal-fired technology, CO_2 emission per kWh generated would be cut by only some 30% compared with today's average coal-fired power station. Natural gas would need to be used in an advanced combined cycle plant to reduce emissions by 75% from today's average.[9]

The UN Framework Convention on Climate Change suggested that CO_2 emissions be limited; the initial target for industrialized countries was to reduce emissions to the 1990 level by 2000 as a first step towards achieving eventual stability of global levels of CO_2 in the atmosphere. As electricity demand may well treble by mid-century (see Table 4.2), that is a difficult target to reach and would imply continuing severe curtailment of emission

---

[9] It should be pointed out that the use of natural gas to combat the greenhouse effect has its limitations. Methane itself is a strong greenhouse gas, and there are concerns about the effect of leakage from natural gas pipelines. See M. Grubb et al., *Energy Policies and the Greenhouse Effect Vol. II: Country Studies and Technical Options*, RIIA/Dartmouth, Aldershot UK. 1991, Appendix 2.4.

beyond 2000. Nuclear energy can be of great benefit. This is already evident from an examination of CO_2 emissions from electricity generation in EC countries. This fell during the 1980s as nuclear production increased and would have been some 35% higher in 1990 if nuclear power had been replaced by fossil fuels. As few new nuclear stations are coming into operation during the 1990s, CO_2 emission is now increasing again.[10] Clearly, the greater the concern to reduce CO_2 emission, the greater the advantage for nuclear power.

It has, however, to be noted that there is still reasonable scientific doubt about the likely extent and impact of greenhouse warming: indeed, so far the Climate Convention requires only rather modest 'precautionary measures'.[11] Convincing evidence one way or the other may emerge over the next ten years or so. It is therefore possible that at that time the greenhouse gas problem will become far more or far less important. In the meantime, decisions on fuel choice must take the CO_2 question into account.

Problems Apart from the question of safety, which is considered below, the perceived environmental problems relate mainly to the fact that the nuclear fuel cycle is not closed and there is no agreement in sight how it should be closed. In the first place, there is considerable controversy about the benefits of reprocessing.[12] Some countries, such as Sweden, Canada and the US, have opted against reprocessing; some, like France and Japan, are in favour of it; and yet others, such as Germany,[13] are reviewing their policy, having decided some years ago to require utilities to arrange for reprocessing. Two issues are involved. The first relates to the question of whether reprocessing makes disposal of waste easier by reducing the volume of HLW or more dangerous by making possible the accidental release of gaseous or liquid radioactive streams into the environment. The second relates to plutonium, which has the reputa-

---

[10] H.D. Schilling, 'Status and Future Prospects of Electricity Generation in Germany', VGB Technical Association of Large Power Plant Operators, Germany, Paper given to the International Symposium on Improved Technology for Fossil Power Plants, Washington DC, March 1993.

[11] M. Grubb et al., *The Earth Summit Agreements*, RIIA/Earthscan, London, 1993, Chapter 6.

[12] 'World Status Report: Plutonium', *FT Energy Economist*, No. 127, London, 18 May 1992, p. 18.

[13] Q. Peel, 'Accord on future of nuclear power industry' and 'Doubts over German nuclear industry', *Financial Times*, 25 and 27 October 1993.

tion with much of the public (whether deserved or not is another subject of passionate debate) of being 'one of the most dangerous substances known to man'. There is also now grave concern in many quarters about what to do with the plutonium from reprocessing, as present plans indicate that a considerable surplus of plutonium is likely to build up.[14] Although there have been many debates about schemes for keeping plutonium stocks under strict international control in the IAEA, so far no agreement has been reached, nor have any moves been seen to implement plans which had been under debate in the EC and the IAEA to control production of plutonium to the level of current usage, even though the US has expressed increasing concern about this build-up.

The second problem with the nuclear fuel cycle is that radioactive waste disposal has become a highly sensitive political issue in many countries; indeed, it has been called the 'Achilles heel' of the nuclear industry. As already mentioned in Chapter 2, there are no permanent disposal facilities for HLW and the slow and cautious work in a number of countries to determine the best and most politically acceptable method of disposal[15] is unlikely to yield results for ten to twenty years. Even finding sites for LLW which are acceptable to the local population is causing severe problems in many countries.

These issues undoubtedly increase the risk of choosing nuclear energy. There could be incidents causing worldwide concern about plutonium handling and/ or temporary storage,[16] leading to a further increase in public hostility to nuclear energy and hence to more stringent government regulations which could increase costs. Such issues are also excellent opportunities for anti-nuclear organizations to strengthen the effectiveness of their opposition.

The nuclear option thus involves a number of considerable uncertainties which are unlikely to be resolved until well into the first decade of the next century. Whether one believes that these uncertainties will resolve themselves in favour of or against nuclear energy is a matter of individual conviction and

---

[14] D. Albright, F. Berkhout and W. Walker, *World Inventory of Plutonium and Highly Enriched Uranium, 1992,* SIPRI/Oxford University Press, 1993, Chapter 5.

[15] R. Kemp, *The Politics of Radioactive Waste Disposal,* Manchester University Press, Manchester, 1992.

[16] See, for example, J. Willman, 'Watchdog Deplores State of Nuclear Stores', *The Financial Times,* 11 October 1993.

belief regarding human society and 'the benevolence of nature', rather than of currently available facts.

(c) Safety risks

Concern about serious accidents at power stations is obviously one of the risks to be considered. Rather against received wisdom, the evidence so far does not indicate nuclear energy to be more risky than other forms of fuel. A study by the UK Health and Safety Executive (HSE)[17] in 1980 concluded that when looking at the whole fuel cycle for coal, oil and nuclear power, the total risks of each are broadly similar. A further report[18] states that plant design acceptable to the Nuclear Installation Inspectorate should ensure that people living near a nuclear power plant in the UK would be exposed to a risk of death from an accidental release of radioactivity of less than one in a million per annum. Similarly, recent information from the US indicates that frequency estimates of catastrophic release of radioactive materials (assessed by the national regulators, not the industry) would under US operating conditions be one in a million per reactor year for the latest LWR designs; that is set to be ten times safer than most present designs of US reactors. The industry's argument that such a level of safety is surely satisfactory has a great deal of force.

Unfortunately, these points do not remove concerns about accidents. The HSE qualifies its conclusions, limiting them to 'suitably sited, constructed and maintained nuclear systems'; and the US presupposes US operating conditions, which are strictly monitored by the nuclear regulatory authorities. No indication can therefore be given about the frequency one could expect for reactors of the same design, but built under inadequate supervision in a country ruled by (say) a military dictatorship and/or if the quality of the operating management in charge of the site and the quality of maintenance were low. As has been shown in other highly reputable industries, slack management leads to insufficient attention to the discipline necessary for safe

---

[17] A.V. Cohen and D.K. Pritchard, *Comparative Risks of Electricity Production Systems: a Critical Survey of the Literature'*, Health and Safety Executive Research Paper No. 11, HMSO, London, 1980.
[18] HSE Working Group, *The Tolerability of Risk from Nuclear Power Stations*, Health and Safety Executive Report, HMSO, London, 1992.

operation, which in turn leads to serious accidents. Piper Alpha, Seveso, Bhopal and the Exxon Valdez were examples of such accidents.

Naturally, companies considering building nuclear power stations will presume that they can build, operate and maintain such units to the required high standard. The risk to them will lie in the possibility that accidents involving nuclear installations anywhere in the world, but especially in industrialized countries, will result in demands by regulatory authorities for costly changes in design and in operating procedure, as happened in the US after the Three Mile Island accident and to the offshore oil industry after the Piper Alpha fire. There is no such risk for fossil fuel power stations.

It is worth pointing out that on past evidence hydroelectric dams may well be the most dangerous form of power generation (with one accident alone causing 12,000 deaths); yet objections against dams seem to concentrate on their effect on the environment rather than on safety (perhaps another example of the perverse perception of risk by the public).

(d) Political risk

It will already have become clear that many of the uncertainties mentioned so far are related to future government judgments and actions, which in turn are much affected by public opinion, particularly, of course, in a democracy. Environmental and safety standards, control of nuclear waste, the decision whether or not to reprocess spent fuel, energy security, the structure of the electricity market, support for nuclear energy, and many other issues are all matters of concern to governments and in some instances matters of international agreements. Governments, however, react to events and to public pressure; thus firm irrevocable policy one year can change into quite the opposite firm irrevocable policy the next.

To take one example, during the 1960s conventional wisdom showed clearly that oil would be a very cheap fuel for power generation for quite some time. Therefore, governments found decisions to base new capacity on that fuel easy to defend and relatively risk-free. After the oil shock of 1973, perception suddenly changed and oil was seen by many as an expensive and insecure fuel. Nuclear energy appeared a more acceptable choice, and many countries decided to make it the central pivot of their energy policy. It quickly fell out of political favour owing to public mistrust on grounds of safety and by the next decade some countries (e.g. Sweden) decided to phase out nuclear energy altogether. Since that time even these decisions have been altered or diluted, often as a result of changes of political parties in power. Other countries, however, such as France and Japan, have so far stuck to their pro-nuclear policies.

An interesting topical example of particular relevance to this study relates to Japan's determination to continue its strategy of achieving greater energy security by recycling plutonium, first via MOX and later by building FBRs,[19] despite doubts expressed by local groups and opponents abroad about the economic need for and political desirability of such plans.[20] Although Japan is presently reviewing its programme,[21] there are so far no indications of change. Clearly, different assumptions lead to different answers, but the possibility of a change of mind in future by one faction or the other cannot be ruled out. One of the few firm predictions about the future is that many *volte-faces* will occur in many countries owing to changing circumstances and national and international pressures.

How far environmental issues are treated seriously is also far more a matter of politics than of economics or science. Thus in Germany, because of the strength of the environmental lobby, controls of sulphur and NOx emissions were treated very seriously and utilities had to spend large sums to meet requirements. In the UK, on the other hand, the political strength of the lobby was far lower and the industry managed to get by with creative calculations and lower expenditure. The UN Convention on Climate Change[22] includes the phrase '. . . that policies and measures to deal with climate change should be cost-effective'. Taking into account the impossibility of ever establishing the true benefit of any individual action, this wording makes it possible for any country to interpret the Convention in any way it sees fit and finds acceptable to its public. The political process has governed decisions of the past

---

[19] Ministry of Foreign Affairs, 'Plutonium, A Renewable Source of Energy: Japan's Policy for Use and Plan for Transport of Plutonium', Tokyo, November 1992; Hiroto Ishida, 'International Understanding for Plutonium Recycling Policy', *Plutonium*, No. 2, August 1993, p. 2.

[20] J. Takagi, 'Recent Plutonium Issues in Japan', Citizens' Nuclear Information Centre, Tokyo, August 1993; D. Swinbanks, 'Japan Debates Plutonium', *Nature*, 7, 352, July 1991.

[21] R. Imai, 'Why the Japanese are Reappraising their Long Term Plans', *Nuclear Engineering International*, November 1992, p. 38.

[22] Grubb et al., *The Earth Summit Agreements*, op. cit.

and there are no signs that this will change, even though ownership of the industry and pressures for competition may make it appear so.

(e) Economic risks

Within most business organizations and in areas where decisions are subject to public discussion, it has been, and still is, the fashion to show that decisions are the outcome of economic calculations, comparing different means of achieving the desired aim and choosing the optimum. Unfortunately, experience in the energy field over many decades has shown the futility of basing decisions on the outcome of such calculations, especially when they involve assessments of project costs for processes not yet developed, as well as guesses about required return on capital and about energy prices over a period of decades. The bases of all such work are forecasts and, as indicated above, these generally prove to be wrong. However, experience has also shown that economic calculations and comparative analyses can play a necessary role in improving judgment by showing the effect of different assumptions, thereby making it possible to identify and concentrate debate on the most important assumptions. Economic analyses become dangerous, however, when used as the main basis for choice.

A consideration of comparative economic advantage has to take into account very many factors and only a few are looked at here. These are capital cost, construction time, unit cost and how projects based on the various fuels might fit different types of electricity markets.

Capital cost and project time   Table 5.1 gives some data on these. The capital cost data for nuclear plants completed since the mid-1980s vary widely, with France and Korea just above $2,000/kW, but with some other countries far higher. The Sizewell B plant in the UK is due to cost some $4,000/kW, but this includes some special factors, such as long delays before authorization and a series of design changes; the utility company concerned (Nuclear Electric) has indicated that in a follow-up project a reduction of some 30% (to around $2,800) could be achieved.[23] Whatever the unreliability of much

---

[23] Institution of Civil Engineers Energy Board, 'Future of the UK Nuclear Industry', ICE, London, 1992.

Table 5.1 Capital costs and project time for generating plant

	Fuel		
	Gas[1]	Coal[1]	Nuclear[2]
Capital cost ($/kW)	500–700	900–1300	2000+
Project time, years			
Pre-construction	1	1–2	2
Construction	2	4–5	6–7
Total	3	5–7	8–9

Sources:
[1] Gainey, *Natural Gas and Power Generation*, Shell International Petroleum Co., 1991; and Tissot and Valais, 'World Gas Supply for the Future', Institut Français du Pétrole, June 1993. Capital cost for gas assumes combined cycle plant; for coal, pulverized coal plant fitted with desulphurizing equipment. Project times are author's own estimates, based on new sites with pre-construction time including planning permission, project negotiation and initial design.
[2] Based largely on Thomas, *Realities of Nuclear Power*, Cambridge University Press, 1988; MacKerron, 'Nuclear costs: why do they keep rising?', *Energy Policy*, 641, July 1992; and Chung-Tek Park, 'The experience of nuclear power development in the Republic of Korea', *Energy Policy*, *721*, August 1992.

of the data, there is reasonable evidence that gas-fired stations are far less capital-intensive than coal-fired ones and that nuclear stations may be between 30% and 50% more costly than coal-fired ones. In addition, the effect of scale on the capital cost/unit is far lower for gas than for nuclear power, with coal in between. As a result, gas stations of 250 MWe or even less can be competitive with larger gas-fired units, while the optimum scale for presently available designs of nuclear units may lie above 1 GWe.

When it comes to unit cost, comparative costs for power from different fuels depends so much on how they have been calculated and on the assumptions made for individual projects, such as discount rate used, price of fuel and type of contract, yearly operating level, cost of nuclear waste disposal and treatment of dismantling costs, that comparisons between data from different sources are meaningless unless all details of the individual calculations are available, and that is rarely the case. The only comment worth making for the purpose of this section is that with today's technology, and with coal at about $50/t ($9/boe) a coal-fired station might have the competitive edge over a nuclear station with a discount rate of 10%, but that the advantage would be reversed with a discount rate of, say, below 5%.[24] Furthermore at the price of gas common in Europe in the early 1990s – around $0.11/m³ ($17.5/boe) – that fuel has a tremendous advantage compared to most other energy forms; indeed, gas prices could double and new gas stations would still remain competitive compared with investing in new coal or nuclear energy.[25] However, for reasons given earlier, there is need of a 'health warning' about *any* comparative cost figures between different sources of energy (particularly over long periods when energy reserves, demand, prices, infrastructure, politics and environmental conditions may change substantially).

If the future costs of power generation projects are full of uncertainties and risks, the income – dependent on the yearly amount of units generated and the price realized for them – is even more difficult to ascertain. It will depend on the structure of the electricity industry in a particular country, what competition there is within that, the regulatory mechanism (if any) controlling the market and what opportunities there may be for importing or exporting electricity to/from other markets. As already mentioned, the past decade has seen major changes in these structures,[26] and there are at present no clear indications of how far these changes will go, or even whether some of them will stand the test of time. Notwithstanding such uncertainties, a project team for a new power generation scheme has to provide a case acceptable to its management and most probably also to banks and other lending institutions to ensure funding. That is no mean task, especially if a nuclear project is involved, possibly costing $2-3 billion with the first income 8 to 9 years away and probably needing expenditure of $200-300 million even before the project can be sufficiently firm for final approval.

---

[24] P. Barnes, 'The OIES Review of Energy Costs', The Oxford Institute for Energy Studies, OIES Review Series, March 1991; 'The Cost of Nuclear Electricity', Briefing Note from Nuclear Electric PLC, February 1993.

[25] B. Tissot and M. Valais, 'World Gas Supply for the Future', Institut Français du Pétrole, June 1993, Section 4.2.

[26] J. Chesshire, 'Why Nuclear Power Failed the Market Test in the UK', *Energy Policy*, 20, August 1992, p. 744.

Of course, such large-scale and long term projects are well known within the energy industry. Natural gas pipelines, liquefied natural gas (LNG) export schemes and offshore oilfield development all need similar expenditures and lead times. For natural gas schemes, experience has shown that such projects only become fundable once there are firm long-term contracts for a substantial portion of the gas, with agreed prices and price escalation clauses. For oil projects, such contracts are rare because there is a large international market in oil and the development of one field is unlikely to change the structure of that market. It also tends to be assumed that the level of international oil prices will continue to be set by political bargaining, whether through OPEC, as today, or by other means, and so be kept well above the cost of producing an additional barrel of oil, which for many fields is likely to lie in the $2-5/bbl range. Because of the high risks of such large energy projects, investors aim for higher than average returns, and authorities generally accept the need for this if such schemes are to be funded. Presumably the same solution could be devised for nuclear power stations, but this would yet again depend on a government's decision that it wishes to provide incentives to attract nuclear power.

Summarizing the economic risk, it seems that nuclear energy would only become a reasonably secure choice if it were backed by government. That is indeed today's situation, as the only countries continuing with the expansion of nuclear power, such as France, Japan, Korea and China, either take centralized decisions about power projects or have governments which are known to be very supportive of nuclear power.

5.4 The impact of market structure

Three examples provide a feel for how different market structures might affect a nuclear project. The first assumes a structure whereby government decides electricity policy, including price, capacity and fuel mix. The second looks at a position where a utility is given a franchise area within which it has the right and the duty to supply customers' demand. As this implies a monopoly position for the vertically integrated supplier, there has to be a regulatory authority to ensure that costs passed through are 'reasonable' (called the 'prudency' test in the US) and that profits are at an acceptable level. The third assumes a highly competitive market with a number of generators supplying the market and with no geographic limitation imposed within a country.

(a) Government in control

The development of a project under the first structure is in principle simple. The decisions on when to build, what fuel to use and the price of power sold are taken by the government, which therefore has to take all project risks. As long as a government can make the required funds available, the choice of nuclear energy or other fuels is part of the political process; economic factors play a role, but not necessarily the major one. That has been the situation in all 'command' economies and may well be the situation in most developing countries.

If a private company is involved in the deal, it is likely to take responsibility only for the effective execution of the project and its efficient operation. It would seek an agreement or an 'understanding' with the authorities to ensure adequate recompense for the services and for any capital the company may have to inject and for any losses incurred as the result of changes in government policies. With government carrying the main risks, there would be no need to require a high return.

(b) Vertically integrated utilities with regional monopoly franchises

In the second structure, which perhaps most resembles the position of US utilities, the responsibility for the choice of fuel and the timing of new capacity lies within the utility operator, which is also responsible for the integrity of the electricity network within its region of franchise. As such integrity requires adequate capacity to meet peak demand, the utility has to assess the growth of demand for some years ahead and determine how this could best be met. If it overestimates demand and therefore builds too much capacity, the utility has the flexibility to shut down the plant with the highest avoidable cost and so make room for its new plant. However, the regulator may disallow the pass-through of some costs associated with such over-capacity; equally, if the chosen route turns out to be more expensive than other alternatives, some costs could be disallowed. Such risks are part of the reason why US utilities have stopped ordering nuclear plants.

Bearing in mind the uncertainties in forecasting electricity demand more than a few years ahead and the difficulty of estimating comparative costs for different fuels, it is hard to see what reasons an operator would have in today's circumstances for choosing the nuclear option with its high initial cost, long time-lag and other risks. Only if the regulator were to accept that additional costs would be seen as prudent, and therefore allowed, could the choice of nuclear energy make commercial sense. As the only reason a regulator might accept such a course, which would imply that customers may have to pay more for their power, would be direction from government, the decision to choose the nuclear route would in effect be underwritten by the government. The utility is likely to ensure that many of the risks associated with such a choice – notably insurance against a major accident – are taken on by government either openly – as was done in the US with the Price-Anderson Indemnity Act of 1957, which asssisted the industry's liability insurance against reactor accidents[27] – or in confidential 'understandings' behind closed doors. In countries such as Japan and Korea which have a strong desire for energy self-sufficiency, there has to be a powerful accord between government desires and utilities' plans, and it may well be that such understandings play a significant role in the companies' decision-making.

(c) Market forces rule

A completely competitive electricity market structure does not yet exist, although the UK privatization was a major step towards it and pressures for greater direct access across EC countries' borders may assist further development of such a system. In this structure no one may have the ultimate responsibility for the integrity of the system, i.e. that there is always adequate stand-by capacity to meet peak demand: it may be left instead to the workings of market forces. As potential shortages start to be perceived, a 'capacity charge' is introduced which, it is assumed, will create incentives to build new capacity.

If that is indeed the concept, it could provide a mortal blow to large-scale schemes with long lead times, such as use of nuclear energy. While the market may react to foreseen shortfalls within two to four years, it is hard to

---

[27] For another example see Michael Smith's report 'BNFL Urges Government to Guarantee Costs', *The Financial Times*, 3 February 1994.

believe that it could be much affected by thoughts of shortfalls nearly a decade away. To lock oneself into large and lengthy expenditure, such as for a
nuclear power station, is unlikely to find much support in management cir-
cles of commercial concerns or their lenders, given the vast uncertainties of
future demand and the fact that competitive pressures may well deny achievement of adequate production level or price when the unit finally comes into
operation.

In any case, as has been seen in many other capital-intensive industries (e.g.
petrochemicals), availability of surplus capacity tends to reduce prices towards the level of marginal cost. If such industries fluctuate between surplus
and shortfall, they can hope to recoup losses made in the former period by
profits made in the latter (though often they do not succeed). The electricity
system, however, is only stable when it has permanent spare capacity so as to
be able to meet peak demand; with a number of competitors fighting for
better loading for their plants, it is difficult to visualize a situation in which
electricity prices would reach and remain at levels that would provide an
adequate return for a nuclear station. In such a system the pressure for pur-
chasing in marginal capacity from elsewhere, or if none is available, adding
capacity in the smallest feasible steps and with the shortest possible lead
time, would be intense. Under today's conditions this implies making maximum use of gas[28] or as second priority perhaps retrofit obsolete coal stations
with more efficient coal plant. If a utility finds that it cannot secure competi-
tively priced fuel for a new project, it need not choose a more risky route; it
can just desist from adding more capacity. After all, it has no responsibility to
ensure that the total market is satisfied.

Governments could affect such commercial decisions through direct action
or via the tax system, but we are then back to the position that nuclear energy
is likely to be chosen only if government decides to back this form of energy
and ensures that the equation between risk and reward is acceptable to the
private investor. Without such backing, the investor would under today's conditions have to accept a high risk/low reward project and – under free market
conditions – would have no reason to do so. Perhaps in future it may become

---

[28] I. Glendenning, 'UK Energy Policy: Can we Avoid the Issue any Longer? A nuclear industry view of energy policy', Paper to British Institute of Energy Economics, 6 April 1993.

possible to enter into a major long-term forward 'take or pay' contract for the provision of bulk power, rather as happens with natural gas now, thereby reducing the economic risk of large-scale new capacity; so far there are few signs of such developments and under competitive conditions, as envisaged in such a market structure, it is not easy to find reasons for entering such contracts.

5.5 Conclusion

There can be little doubt that the future of nuclear energy is in the hands of governments, whether they like it or not. If they back the energy form, it will have a future; if only a few do, or even if many stay neutral, the future will be limited at best. What attitude to this energy form would one wish governments and the international community to take?

The Need for Nuclear Power Examined

6.1 Competing fuels for electricity generation

Before examining the future need for nuclear energy it is necessary to consider possible contributions from alternative fuels. The present proportion of electricity generated from various fuels is shown in Table 6.1. This chapter looks at the possible future contributions of the various competitor fuels.

(a) Fossil fuels

Table 6.2 provides a general view of the fossil fuel production, reserve and resource situation. The data in the table are the basis for the later discussions of the individual fuels.

It is important to note that the definition of 'proven reserves' represents quantities about which 'there is reasonable certainty that they can be recovered from known reservoirs *under existing economic and operating conditions'*. Figures for reserves are therefore affected by changes of technology and price. Data for resources are by their nature controversial and the figures in Table 6.2 would be seen by many as falling near the bottom of the range.

(i) Oil
Latest estimates of ultimate resources for recoverable conventional oil seem to fall in the range of 200 to 450 Gt[1] with, as indicated in Table 6.2, far larger resources of shale oil, tar sands and heavy oils; the base is therefore sufficient to support increases in demand for many years to come. However, it is difficult to see the case for an increase in the use of conventional oil for power generation. Although the fuel has specific advantages for transport, it has no obvious ones for power production, and the oil industry may well find it difficult enough to meet the increases in demand for transport fuel. If growth of demand for that sector continues unabated (which would be the case with

---

[1] P. Barnes, 'The Oil Supply Mountain: Is the Summit in Sight?', The Oxford Institute for Energy Studies, OIES Review Series, Oxford, 1993.

Table 6.1 Fuels for electricity generation, 1990

	% contribution to electricity supply		
	Industrialized world	Developing world	Total world
Coal	44	33	42
Oil	9	17	10
Natural gas	12	13	12
Hydroelectric	16	33	18
Nuclear	18	4	17
Other	1	—	1
Total	100	100	100

Note: Industrialized world includes OECD, eastern Europe and the former Soviet Union, the developing world all the rest.

Source: CEC DG XVII, 'A View to the Future', *Energy in Europe*, Special Issue, September 1992.

Table 6.2 Production, reserves and resource of fossil fuels (10^9 toe)

	Oil	Gas	Coal
1990 production	3.15	1.74	2.18
% used in power production	*10*	*18*	*65*
Proven reserves	136.5	107	570
1990 reserves/production ratio, years	43	58	260
Ultimate recoverable resource	200[1]	220[2]	3,400

Notes:

[1] Conventional oil only; unconventional oil, such as heavy crude, tar sands and oil shale would add some 600×10^9 toe.

[2] Conventional gas only; reserves for unconventional gas, such as methane hydrates and geopressured gas, could be far higher.

Source: BP Statistical Review of Energy, 1991, and for resources, World Energy Council, 'Energy for Tomorrow's World', London, 1993, Table 3.2.

a rapid increase of car population in the developing world), it may already be necessary by mid-century to call on unconventional high-cost oil and even on synthetic oil made from tar sands, shale oil or coal. Because of its cost, such 'syncrude' is a most unlikely fuel for power generation.

Conventional oil is likely to be used for electricity generation only where there are special conditions, such as proximity to a source of refinery residues, or for isolated applications, such as islands. It is unlikely to make a signifi-cant contribution to meeting future electricity demand, perhaps falling from today's 10% to 5% by 2020, with further reductions thereafter. There is, however, the possibility of greater use of heavy oils, such as Venezuelan heavy crude, which has recently started to be used as power station fuel, having been transported in the form of water emulsion (Orimulsion). Al-though this is a fuel containing many pollutants, the latest technology can overcome these economically if the price of this fuel is set accordingly. By 2050 such fuels and other unconventional oils could, if economic and pub-licly acceptable, readily match today's proportion of oil burn in power stations.

(ii) Natural gas   Recent technological developments have made natural gas the 'dream fuel' of the electricity industry. In addition to the considerable economic advantages already remarked on above, gas-fired power plants are environmentally clean compared with other fossil fuels, so that gas genera-tion projects tend to be far more acceptable to localities than projects using other fuels.[2]

These are all recent developments which have hardly affected the global contribution of gas in today's power stations. Until now, generation from gas has largely taken place in areas with indigenous natural gas, as well as in Japan, where it became the preferred fuel partly for environmental reasons. As gas turbine-based stations are very flexible and quick to start up, they are used in many power systems to cover peak loads, but beyond that, use has been held back in a number of countries because until recently discriminatory regulations against natural gas for power generation were in force. Since for

---

[2] Concerning the greenhouse effect of this fuel, see M. Grubb et al., *Energy Policies and the Greenhouse Effect Vol. II: Country Studies and Technical Options*, RIIA/Dartmouth, Alder-shot UK, 1991, Appendix 2.4.

the most part these no longer exist, rapid expansion of gas generation is likely to commence in most countries with access to gas supply.

When considering the natural gas resource base, it has to be remembered that until some 20 years ago there was, outside the US, only limited interest in exploration for gas. There now appears to be rapid progress in finding more gas. A recent study of gas resources[3] states these to be about 130Gtoe and the ultimate resource base for conventional natural gas at some 350-450Gtoe, both considerably higher than the data quoted in Table 6.2 above. With demand at some 1.9Gtoe/yr, there appears to be a great deal of room for major expansion into power generation, even taking account of the lower figures in that table. It is all the more likely on the basis of the higher figures and the fact that reserves have been increasing at over 5% p.a. over the past 15 years, and given that estimates of the resource base have doubled over the last 20 years.

There are, however, problems. First, the physical characteristics of natural gas make it difficult and expensive to store and to transport over long distances. Transportation has to be either by pipeline or as LNG, shipped in special tankers from and to highly specialized terminals. As already mentioned earlier, such transportation schemes need to be large and based on firm off-take contracts for a high proportion of the gas. LNG schemes are also inherently dangerous, although the industry has had an excellent safety record. Because each scheme is so large, only experienced and reputable operators tend to be chosen to manage them and these are well aware of the importance of safety.

Secondly, most of the reserves of gas (some 70%) are in the Middle East and Siberia, well away from centres of utilization. That exacerbates the problem of transportation. The third problem, and perhaps the most difficult for the power generation industry, is security of supply. Although there is today ample gas available in the main consuming areas, that position may well not last long once use of gas for power generation takes off. After that, imports from new jumbo supply projects would become necessary. Even though the generating industry may well be able to afford the higher prices needed for

---

[3] B. Tissot and M. Valais, *World Gas Supplies for the Future: Questions and Answers*, Institut Français du Pétrole, 1993.

such projects, these do need a great deal of time to come to fruition and are therefore unlikely to start producing until well into the next decade. Too great a rush for gas could cause supply problems. For the longer term, given the difficulty and cost of storage and that each project will have dedicated customers, the effect of breakdowns or disruption of even one project could cause substantial dislocation to a utility, should it depend on gas from that project for a high proportion of its fuel.

Lastly, many of the countries without their own gas production in the developing world will have far too small an off-take to justify import terminals for LNG, or dedicated pipelines. They may therefore not have the opportunity to make use of this fuel.

Notwithstanding these difficulties, the large technical advantages, the healthy resource base and public acceptability are likely to cause the proportion of gas in the future supply mix for electricity generation to increase considerably. Should gas take up, say, 20% of power generation by mid-century, demand for that purpose would have increased by nearly fivefold from today. Considering the security of supply questions and the high costs of transporting gas to small users, it would be unreasonable to expect much more. If, however, estimates of the resource base continue to increase rapidly and if some of the findings are in highly populated countries like China and India, gas could become an even more important source for power production, probably at the expense of coal. As such a development could well happen, gas should be looked at as a possible joker in the pack.

(iii) Coal   The advantages and disadvantages of coal seem to be the reverse of those of natural gas. With some 42% of electric power presently produced from coal, it is today still the most important fuel for electricity production, which is by far the main use of coal. The world resource base is vast and geographically well distributed. From the resource point of view, coal is, therefore, a very promising fuel to meet the increasing demand for power.

Its disadvantage is that conventional coal-burning plant is more expensive, environmentally dirty and is less efficient than oil- or gas-burning plants. Also coal, when burnt in conventional plants, emits about three times the quantity of CO_2/kWh than the latest natural gas plants. As already remarked, considerable advances have been made over the past decade in developing environmentally acceptable coal-burning plants of higher efficiency, but even these would emit twice as much CO_2 as a gas-fired combined cycle plant.

If the objective of the UN Convention on Climate Change to limit CO_2 emission is to be achieved, developed countries will have to limit their coal burning, perhaps quite severely, to make way for countries like India and China, which have large resources of coal and are unlikely to accept limitations on their freedom to make use of their major energy resource for basic industrialization. Therefore, with the greenhouse effect in mind, it has to be assumed that as electricity demand grows, the proportion produced from coal must drop, possibly to 25% by 2050. Even taking into account increasing efficiency of future coal-fired stations, that would still imply a small increase over today's levels in the volume of coal used for power production.

(b) Renewables and nuclear fusion

Except for nuclear fission, renewable energy sources (which harness the energy of the sun, tides or the earth's heat) and nuclear fusion are the only alternatives to fossil fuels.

(i) Hydroelectricity   This is the only renewable energy resource so far used on a large scale, with about 18% or around 2,200 TWh/yr of world electricity being produced in this way. Capacity in most OECD countries has been stable for quite some time and it may well be that these countries have reached optimum capacity. That is not the case for the former USSR and much of the developing world, where there appears to be considerable exploitable potential, but unfortunately mostly well away from areas of demand. Data from the World Energy Council in 1992[4] estimate an 'exploitable capability' of 10,000 TWh/yr, although some of the sites included in such a figure may under today's more stringent environmental yardsticks be no longer seen as suitable.

Although in the past large hydro schemes were seen as symbols of progress, the latest views are rather more jaundiced because it was found that such schemes can cause substantial environmental damage and severe problems to local inhabitants. Attention is now being focused on smaller hydropower

---

[4] World Energy Council, *1992 Survey of Energy Resources*, 16th edition, WEC, London, 1992.

projects; where large ones are being planned much time is spent on environmental impact studies. Notwithstanding these problems, there is no reason to doubt that hydro capacity will continue to increase, though taking into account the 'exploitable capability', perhaps 5,000 TWh/yr or some 15% of electricity supply by 2050, may be all that can be expected.

(ii) 'New' renewables This section does not include traditional renewable energy sources like wood and dung because these are rarely used for electricity generation. It covers a large number of diverse ways of harnessing 'natural energy' for power generation, such as energy from the sun via thermal or photovoltaic routes, wind and tides, small hydroelectric schemes, the use of biomass from farm residues or from plantation crops, and geothermal energy.

Interest in the concept of 'new' renewable energy started in the early 1970s with the views expressed by the Club of Rome and others that the world might well run short of fossil fuels. Much research and development has been done in this field since and many people working in it have become convinced that this is a major potential energy resource waiting to be tapped. They believe that, when fully developed, it would be competitive with most other forms of energy and would, moreover, be in line with the aim of 'sustainable development' proposed in the Brundtland Report in the 1980s. Others, especially from some major energy utilities, strongly dispute these conclusions and provide quite different economic information. So far, except for some use of agricultural residues, wind energy and small hydroelectric schemes, the utilities have made little commercial use of any such resources; neither side, therefore, has practical experience to back its claims.

Perhaps one reason for the controversies surrounding this area is the fact that most renewable energy projects would be small in relation to the gigawatt projects of conventional power generation. This attracts those who believe that 'small is beautiful' and repels others whose experience tells them that large is more profitable. Each side (naturally) accuses the other of bias. In some areas, seen by enthusiasts as having considerable potential, such as electricity from biomass and the photoelectric routes, one way of resolving the issue would be to test some of the schemes through experience of commercial-scale operation. However, this is expensive and, although public and private organizations are funding development and pilot-scale work, there appears to be little appetite so far for this next step. A strong complaint from the 'renewable lobby' arises from the low priority given to renewable energy for funding development by member countries of the International Energy Agency (IEA). Their national energy research budgets show that 50% goes to nuclear energy, but only 7% to renewables. [5]

It should be noted that not all such renewable sources are environmentally benign. As with large hydroelectric projects, large tidal, wave and wind schemes can cause problems in this area.

A recent study by the World Energy Council[6] indicated that continuation of today's rather slow progress in this field could mean that by 2020 some 10% of global electricity generation would come from a mix of the diverse sources making up this sector, but that this could increase to perhaps 20% if the world were to make determined efforts to speed up such development. Another recent study, sponsored by a United Nations energy group,[7] concluded that as much as 40% of electricity could be generated from this source by 2025 and perhaps 45% by 2050. Although the study is backed up by a great deal of detail, such rapid progress is difficult to believe – not because the data are necessarily suspect, but because a sudden 'conversion' of politicians and industrialists throughout the industrialized countries would be needed to take a new, unproven and risky path involving a great deal of development effort and money for demonstration plant. Nevertheless, there can be little doubt that the potential is there, the technological basis for harnessing it is available and sooner or later funds for the effort to commercialize such development will be forthcoming. The next energy crisis (whether imagined or real) may well be the trigger for such an evolution.

If such a crisis were to come about during the next ten years, or if for one reason or another it were decided to phase out nuclear energy and divert much of the effort from that source to renewables, the higher World Energy Council figure might become possible. It is therefore assumed that renewables could, if necessary, meet between 10% and 25% of electricity demand by

[5] T.B. Johansson et al. (eds), *Renewable Energy: Sources for Fuel and Electricity*, Island Press, Washington DC, 1993, Chapter 1.

[6] WEC Commission, *Energy for Tomorrow's World*, World Energy Council, London, 1993.

[7] Johansson et al. (eds), *Renewable Energy: Sources for Fuel and Electricity*, op. cit.

2020 and at a guess 25% to 40% by 2050, although the author's judgment is that 15% might be a more realistic top figure for 2020.

(iii) Nuclear fusion   When it comes to looking at the future of electric power a number of decades ahead, the question has to be asked whether and by when nuclear fusion could start playing a role. Work on this energy form has been going on since the late 1950s in the hope of being able to harness the energy released when two light atoms (the two hydrogen isotopes, deuterium and tritium) fuse to form a heavier atom, helium. It was hoped that such a reaction would provide a virtually infinite and trouble-free source of energy, as the source of the isotopes would be water and the process might produce far less radioactive waste than nuclear fission. Although so far perhaps as much as $20 billion[8] has been spent on this research, there is still no clear indication whether or not the fusion reaction can be harnessed for commercial power production.

As even the experimental equipment has turned out to be very large and expensive and requires very long lead times, few specialists believe that a fully commercial prototype for nuclear fusion would be ready before the second half of the next century and before the expenditure of at least another $30 billion.[9] When looking at power production up to mid-century, therefore, this source is not relevant.

6.2 The need for nuclear power

It can be seen from the previous section that the total resource base of fossil fuels plus the hydroelectric potential seems ample to meet demand for electricity generation for the next century and possibly well beyond. A number of other factors were also identified, and when these are taken into account by making assumptions such as are outlined below, it is possible to develop a 'feel' for the implications of this information on the split of fuels for future power generation. This is shown in Table 6.3.

---

[8] J. Clark and G. McKerron, 'Great Expectations: A Review of Nuclear Fusion Research', *Energy Policy*, February 1989, p. 49.

[9] 'World Status Report: Fusion Power', *FT Energy Economist*, June 1988, p. 17.

Table 6.3 Electricity supply projections: potential contributions and the need for nuclear power

	1990	Maximum % contribution to supply			
		2020		2050	
CO_2 restrictions		Yes	No	Yes	No
Coal	42	35	40	25	45
Oil*	10	5	10	5	10
Natural gas	12	20	20	20	20
Hydroelectric	18	15	15	15	10
New renewables	1	10–15	10	10–35	10–20
Total	83	85–90	95	75–100	95–100
Resulting Minimum Nuclear Contribution	17	10–15	5	0–25	0–5

*Includes unconventional heavy oil.

Source: For 1990 data, see CEC DG XVII, 'A View to the Future', *Energy in Europe*, Special Issue, September 1992. Rest are author's estimates.

Two scenarios are examined, one assuming that there will be continuing – and perhaps increasing – concern about the greenhouse effect; the other, that by early in the next century this factor will have sunk to lower levels in the world's energy priorities. For both cases, high contributions from fuels other than nuclear are taken, so that the nuclear contribution is the lowest needed to achieve the balance.

Other assumptions are:

Coal: The new cleaner and more efficient coal technology will not be fully commercially proven until beyond the end of this century. This could result in delays in ordering new plant and a dip in the percentage for coal use by 2020.
Gas: Because of the time needed to get large export gas projects from concept to commercial operation, it is assumed that an increase in the use of gas for power generation could be limited by supply considerations.

Oil: By mid-century most of the oil for power generation is assumed to be heavy oils.

Hydro: By 2050, sites for large-scale hydro projects may become difficult to find.

New renewables: Here it is assumed that without special effort, this form would capture some 10% of the power market; but if worries about the greenhouse effect persist, the proportion in later years would depend on perceptions of how successful the development of this energy form would be in comparison with nuclear energy and fossil fuels.

If the figures in Table 6.3 are taken at their face value, the implications would be as follows:

(1) With CO_2 restraint, there is, from the point of view of supply security, a strong case for persevering with the nuclear option. Without this option, dependence on renewables would be very great. This is surely a high-risk strategy, bearing in mind today's lack of experience with these sources. Conversely, without a significant input from renewables, we would be too dependent on the nuclear option. It is, therefore, not a matter of continuing with either one or the other source, but with both.

(2) There seems to be no case for a vast and rapid expansion of nuclear energy. Continuation of around today's proportion of some 15%+, implying moderate, but steady growth of capacity, would certainly suffice until 2020.

(3) Without the greenhouse constraints, the need for nuclear energy is weak. A slow run-down as nuclear stations reach the end of their operating life, acceleration of coal and heavy oil use plus a steady advance of renewables could easily balance the supply/demand equation.

Table 6.3 is quite inadequate as a basis for looking at the future of nuclear energy, and would be so even if it were based on the consensus view of a number of experts, rather than on the guesses of one individual. Two reasons for this are paramount:

First, the world cannot be treated as one homogeneous block. Choice of fuel for power stations is in the hands of many individual utilities and governments, each with different interests and constraints, amongst which the total future world energy balance may be a very minor consideration. Whether the world balance needs nuclear power or not, France and Japan are, on present indications, unlikely to change their nuclear policies, nor would US utilities recommence ordering nuclear plant, unless conditions changed in such a way as to make them consider such action to be in their own interest. All one can hope for is that individual decisions will be taken with an eye to the global situation.

The second reason is uncertainty. Perceptions change and it would be quite irrational to assume that today's views will stay unchanged for the next twenty years. As already mentioned, forecasts must be treated with great suspicion and are by themselves a bad basis for long-term decisions. It could be that in x years' time the concern about climate change becomes so great that fossil fuel burning will be very severely constrained in many countries, thus making nuclear energy and renewables far more important. It is also possible that worries about nuclear terrorism and safety will increase to such an extent that people decide it is better to cope with climate change than face the perceived dangers of large-scale nuclear power. Similarly, the demand level could be inaccurate by plus or minus 20% or more; technological advances or price movements could change the relative economics of fuels; the political pressure for self-sufficiency could increase or disappear, and so on.

Despite such vast uncertainties, decisions have to be taken. These should be of a kind that does not lock the world into dangerous or regretted courses of action, but still ensures availability of adequate and affordable energy. Of course, firm, irrevocable action to deal with an (apparently) foreseeable future may seem better than keeping one's options open, but only if that future actually comes about. If it does not, as is normally the case, especially in the energy field, there can be serious trouble. Having seen throughout history the failure of many fortifications because they faced the wrong way, military strategists are only too well aware of such dangers.

Napoleon's dictum 'Unhappy the general who comes on the field of battle with a plan' is as relevant to the energy strategist as it is to defence planners. The implication for energy planning should be in the direction of avoiding too great a dependence on one plan, but making certain that the ability to carry out one of a series of alternative options rapidly and efficiently is available when the case for that particular option becomes clear.

What is the effect of such thinking on the need for nuclear power? Obviously, making and implementing a decision either to phase it out abruptly or to start a major and rapid expansion should be avoided until we are far more certain whether either is the right course to follow. That may be in one, two or more decades, but in the meantime we have to monitor the situation so as to be able to judge when such a decision – or another – becomes necessary. In other words, we have today inadequate information to judge whether or not there is a future need for nuclear power. When the time for such a policy decision comes, the ability must be available to carry it out quickly and effectively by having the technology and all the other means needed for implementation in readiness.

The implications for nuclear energy and the question as to whether we would be ready for such a decision, if it could be made shortly, will be examined in Chapter 7. This will consider three cases:

(1) Worldwide phasing out of nuclear energy, though without panic measures entailing the closure of viable power stations.
(2) Continuation of today's situation, with enthusiasm for the energy form in some countries and a distinct lack of enthusiasm in others.
(3) Worldwide expansion, leading to a marked effect on global CO_2 emissions by mid-century.

Nuclear Options

Although the three cases outlined at the end of Chapter 6 are illustrative only, it is possible to make a rationale for them:

Case 1 Phase out – assumes that nuclear energy is judged too expensive/ dangerous and should be phased out as soon as practicable. Here there are two possibilities to consider; namely, a rapid closure of most nuclear facilities in the civil domain; or a slower 'fade-out' whereby nuclear plants at the end of their life would not be replaced, which would prolong phasing out until well beyond 2020.

Case 2 Present situation continues – assumes that some countries, such as France, Japan and Korea will continue nuclear expansion and may be joined by a few more, say from East Asia, but that others will either phase out deliberately or not replace redundant capacity for economic or political reasons. Under such circumstances, nuclear capacity might increase slowly from today's level of 360 GWe, perhaps to 500 GWe by mid-century.

Case 3 Worldwide expansion – assumes that the greenhouse effect is confirmed and that renewables, though making a contribution, do not come up to the expectation of enthusiasts. The proportion of nuclear-generated electricity reaches 25% by 2050, implying a capacity of 1,400-1,500 GWe by then.

The relevant nuclear generating capacity for each case is shown in Figure 7.1, while the implications of these options and the requirements to make them realistic are discussed below.

Figure 7.1 Total nuclear generating capacity for the three cases, 1970–2050

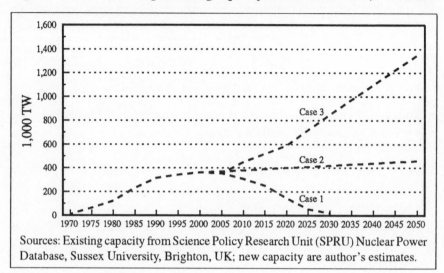

Sources: Existing capacity from Science Policy Research Unit (SPRU) Nuclear Power Database, Sussex University, Brighton, UK; new capacity are author's estimates.

7.1 Case 1: Phase-out

Phase-out is clearly the preferred choice of the more simplistic adherents of the anti-nuclear lobby: 'Let us close all plants as soon as practicable and in due course forget all about this failed experiment.' Reality is, unfortunately, more complex. First, we cannot 'de-invent' nuclear technology, nor can we forget about all the nuclear waste and radioactive plant left behind. Secondly, who decides? Although some countries, such as Sweden, have decided to phase out nuclear energy (though only slowly and even that is not certain), others are continuing to believe in and expand nuclear power. How can the believers in a nuclear future be forced to abandon their strategies? It would need at least another serious and headline-grabbing accident to make up the collective international mind to agree to such a phase-out and make real attempts to enforce it, although how this might be done is not at all clear. Even if agreed upon, implementation cannot be quick; countries would have to find alternative means of meeting their power demand, and where nuclear energy provides over 50% of demand, that could take decades. Thus the option of deliberate and rapid phasing out worldwide is not realistic and is unlikely ever to be so.

More easy to envisage is a case where individual nuclear reactors, when at the end of their life, are mostly replaced by non-nuclear facilities, so shrinking the importance of nuclear power, until within a few decades it would no longer be worthwhile to keep the industry up to date. By that is meant that the continuous effort to utilize operational experience to improve the reliability, safety and economics of an industry – a matter which is especially essential in such a complex high-technology field as nuclear energy – would become inadequate to keep the industry healthy.

One can see such a case arising, possibly even in quite a fortuitous way. As already mentioned in Chapter 5, it is, under present circumstances, difficult to see private operators deliberately choosing nuclear power generation, unless government not only supports such a choice but underwrites many of the risks that are specific to nuclear energy. If present trends to bring greater competition into the electricity market, together with public mistrust of nuclear energy, continue, individual governments may meet political resistance when trying to agree adequate incentives to entice potential investors into nuclear projects. Assistance for other energies, such as renewables, could become politically easier. Over time, therefore, there could be a slow run-down of nuclear capacity by default. Even if some countries stood out against such a trend and were to continue to invest in nuclear plant, the industry would soon lose its critical mass and slowly decline.

Of course, the main unresolved issue of today – how best to deal with nuclear waste – would still require resolution. By 2010, spent fuel in temporary storage might amount to some 300,000 tonnes,[1] containing perhaps some 2,000 tonnes of plutonium, scattered throughout 30 or more countries. If all goes well, perhaps the first permanent depository for HLW might be completed by then, but permanent storage for the rest, safe for many thousands of years, would still have to be found. In addition, all the facilities which handled radioactive materials would have to be dismantled and made safe, a process which is likely to take many decades. Long after power generation has stopped, someone will still have to find substantial sums of money to ensure such long-term security.

---

[1] D. Albright, F. Berkhout and W. Walker, *World Inventory of Plutonium and Highly Enriched Uranium, 1992,* SIPRI/Oxford University Press, 1993, Chapter 5.

That, unfortunately, is not the whole picture about waste. In addition to waste from the civil programme, there is also waste from the military programmes. As the US has over 600,000m^3 of HLW (including transuranic[2] waste)[3] and Russia possibly even more, the totals from the weapons programme dwarf the quantity of civil waste. Sooner or later something has to be done with this waste to ensure it will not remain a major hazard for many tens of generations. For reasons discussed below, this might be easier to achieve on the back of a flourishing civil industry which has resolved its waste disposal problems, than just as a 'one off' military clean-up issue.

In summary, the option of phasing out would not stop the need to resolve today's concerns about safety and security. Even if there were no power generation, a nuclear industry of some sort would have to be with us for perhaps a century or more to ensure that waste (including dismantled nuclear plant and military waste) from all the countries with nuclear facilities was safely disposed of. Paradoxically, such an industry might well become more accident-prone, the smaller it became. As no one likes to work in a dying field, the quality of new recruits and of management (which tends to directly affect the level of safe operation) within the industry might well deteriorate, while funds to ensure adequate safety might become harder and harder to find.

7.2 Case 2: Continuation of the present situation

Considering present controversies about nuclear energy, this is the most likely case, at least for this decade and perhaps even the next. It assumes that some countries and some utilities will continue to support nuclear energy, while others will replace plant which has reached the end of its economic life with non-nuclear capacity. It also assumes that with few exceptions, mainly in East Asia, the developing world will be slow to choose nuclear power because the current types of reactor are not well suited for their purpose and because, with continuing concerns about safety and proliferation, interna-

---

[2] Transuranic elements are those with an atomic number greater than that of uranium (which is 92) and include plutonium and other long-lived fission products.
[3] J.D. Werner, 'Plutonium: Environmental Impact and Constraints', in M. Grubb, R. Garwin and E. Matanle (eds), *Managing the Plutonium Surplus: Applications and Technical Options*, NATO/Kluwer, forthcoming 1994.

tional lenders, already concerned about the economics, may feel even less keen than today to sponsor nuclear power for such countries. The general effect of such moves might be that overall nuclear capacity could stay steady for the next decade at about today's capacity of 360 GWe and subsequently creep up slowly, say to 450-500 GWe within 30 to 50 years. The proportion of world nuclear power generation would thus drop, perhaps to below 10% in the 2020s.

Depending on the nuclear industry's perception of this case, there are two alternatives to be looked at. If the industry continues to hope and work for a breakthrough to the 'big time', such as global expansion, it will undoubtedly continue to try to make the technology more acceptable to utilities, governments and – perhaps most important – the public. It is therefore likely to persist with the development of more economic and simpler reactors, greater safety, technically and politically acceptable ways of overcoming waste problems, and ways of dealing with the dangers of proliferation.

There is also the possibility that much of the industry will have stopped believing in such a breakthrough and be ready to accept the role of a modest player in the energy supply field. Under such circumstances, major development efforts are unlikely. This would mean, just as in Case 1, that there would be fewer resources available to resolve the outstanding issues from the civil and military programmes. It may well be that this alternative may slowly slip into a phase-out. In other words, the present situation cannot continue for long, unless it is seen by the industry and its proponents as a stepping-stone to a greater future. The complexity, international nature and costs of nuclear technology, as available today, plus the long time-spans needed for development, make it unsuited to a minor role in the global energy scene.

7.3 Case 3: Worldwide expansion

Although, as already indicated in Chapter 6, there is no case for an early decision on a major global expansion programme for nuclear power, this third scenario assumes – quite arbitrarily – that general agreement for such an expansion is reached before the end of this century. It is assumed that by 2050, we could achieve a 25% nuclear contribution to worldwide electricity generation. Such a proportion coming from nuclear energy, together with an increased contribution from renewables and the availability of more efficient fossil fuel generating plant, should make it possible to produce three times more power in 2050 than in 1990 with only a 30% increase in CO_2 emission from power generation.

Until 2020, the rate of expansion in installed operating capacity is likely to be constrained by the need for the construction, design and fabrication industry to gear itself for high growth after the low level of today's activities. With decisions to expand coming towards the end of this decade, little additional new capacity would come on-stream until well into the first decade of the new century and the total new capacity in the first 20 years might only be around 400 GWe. With around 140 GWe of pre-2000 capacity[4] still operating by 2020, maximum total capacity by then might be no higher than 550-600 GWe, which could provide about the same proportion of electric power as today. Such a constraint should not apply for the period thereafter, so that faster expansion between 2020 and 2050 is assumed in the option. It is also assumed that the rate of construction of nuclear power plants in the developing world will lag behind that in the industrialized countries for a few decades. Table 7.1 shows capacity and material flows for such a case and Figure 7.2 shows the capacity data in diagrammatic form.

When considering the feasibility of this option, a number of questions come to mind about world uranium resources, waste disposal and reprocessing.

(a) *The uranium resource*
Perhaps the first question to look at is whether the option would force the world into plutonium recycling and therefore reprocessing on a major scale and if so, when. This depends in the first instance on views about world uranium resources.

Uranium resources are usually quoted as 'known resources', with a defined production cost. For a cost of less than $130/kg, these are presently estimated to be some 3.7 million tonnes. As already indicated when discussing fossil fuel resources (6.1 above), such data can be highly misleading when looking at the longer-term supply position. Uranium availability has been in substantial surplus over the past 15 years and spot prices during the period

---

[4] SPRU Nuclear Power Database, Sussex University, Brighton, UK.

Table 7.1 Nuclear power generation under worldwide expansion

	1990			2020			2050		
	IW[a]	DW	Total	IW	DW	Total	IW	DW	Total
Total demand, TWh x 10³	9.0	2.6	11.6	13.0	10.0	23.0	14.6	21.1	35.7
Proportion produced from Nuclear %	18	4	17	22	10	17	35	18	25
Net nuclear capacity GWe[b]	300	15	315	440	150	590	800	550	1350
Natural uranium need t/yr x 10³			50			90			200
Spent fuel make t/yr HM[c] x 10³			8	9	3	12	16	11	27
Plutonium in spent fuel t/yr			60	90	30	120	160	110	270

Notes:

[a] Industrialized world includes OECD, eastern Europe and the former Soviet Union only; the developing world is all the rest.

[b] Assumes a load factor of 75%. Assuming also that the size of future nuclear reactors will average around 1 GWe, the figures for 'capacity needed' translates itself into the approximate number of reactors needed.

[c] HM = Heavy Metal in spent fuel, comprising uranium, plutonium and transuranic fission products.

Source: Total demand from Table 4.2, nuclear proportion beyond 1990 are author's estimates, yearly quantities based on Uranium Institute fact sheet 'Radioactive Waste and the Nuclear Fuel Cycle', London, August 1992.

Figure 7.2 World generating capacity, GWe, and percentage nuclear share of capacity

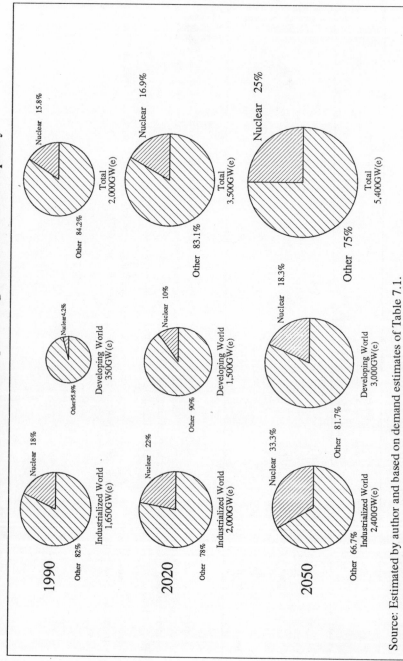

Source: Estimated by author and based on demand estimates of Table 7.1.

fell from some \$65/kg to below \$25/kg. In such circumstances, there was little incentive to explore for more reserves, but that does not imply that more cannot be found when the industry has an incentive to find more. With the experience of the oil industry in mind, where in the past 50 years reserve/ production ratios have increased from 20 years to 40 years today, even though demand is now eight times larger, a recent estimate of an ultimate recoverable resource base of 17 million tonnes at less than \$130/kg uranium[5] seems far more realistic.

Because of the present surplus of uranium, there is at present no incentive to increase the 'known resource', but even the present 'known resources' of 3.7 million tonnes indicate ample availability for at least 30 years. Under the option considered here, demand would start picking up by around 2020 to a level at which exploration might again become of interest, so that there could be a better idea of reserves and resources by 2030. Without plutonium recycling, the option would imply total use of around 6 million tonnes of uranium over the first half of the next century and a need for some 200,000 t/yr by 2050. If the resource of 17 million tonnes is found to be of the right order, there is ample uranium for this option, and any case for reprocessing and use of the fast breeder reactor cannot be based on a possible uranium shortage, at least until well into the second half of the next century. On the other hand, if, by 2020, uranium is seen to be more scarce, reprocessing plants may be needed by mid-century.

Such a view of the uranium resource does not take supply security of individual countries into account. Although uranium resources are more widely distributed than oil, this issue is of concern to some countries (e.g. Japan) and makes them more interested in aiming for reprocessing and plutonium recycling.

(b) Management of waste
A further question to consider is the destination of the nuclear waste from such a programme. The (very approximate) amounts of spent fuel, in terms of heavy metal, that are produced are shown in Table 7.2.

---

[5] WEC Commission, *Energy for Tomorrow's World*, World Energy Council, London, 1993, Table 3.3.

Table 7.2 High level nuclear waste production under worldwide expansion (Case 3)

	Tonnes HM/yr	Cumulative from 1960, tonnes HM*
1990	8,000	115,000
2020	12,000	450,000
2050	27,000	1,100,000

*To this cumulative total has to be added more that 1 million cubic metres of military waste (HM tonnage equivalent unknown).

It is presently assumed that the spent fuel will be stored in interim facilities, normally at reactor sites, for at least 20 years. Beyond that time, the fuel would either have to be disposed of in permanent repositories or reprocessed to reclaim plutonium and uranium for re-use in fresh fuel. If reprocessed, the long-lived high-level waste, mainly fission products other than plutonium, is concentrated and will have to be sent to permanent HLW repositories, possibly after several more decades of temporary storage.

By 2020 some 250,000 tonnes of spent fuel should be ready for disposal or reprocessing. As it is presently assumed that each HLW depository might be limited to the storage of around 70,000 tonnes spent fuel,[6] or the equivalent concentrated HLW waste from reprocessing, some three or four depositories might be needed by then. (The storage limitation stated is set by the heat release of the fission products and is not a volume factor; a full depository would be equivalent to a heat source of 10 MW. As plutonium is not a major contributor to heat release, it is believed in some quarters that reprocessing and concentrating the high heat-release fission products into a far smaller volume may not greatly affect the number of repositories needed.)

Although many countries are developing schemes for such repositories, few are likely to be in operation before 2020[7] and there is presently no indication whether countries will be willing to take others' waste. In practice,

---

[6] W. Häfele, 'Energy from Nuclear Power', *Scientific American*, September 1990, p. 91.
[7] W. Häfele, 'On the Nature of Nuclear Power and its Future', Rossendorf Research Centre, Dresden. Paper given to Global 93 Conference, Seattle, US, September 1993.

therefore, some of the spent fuel would have to spend far longer in temporary storage.

On the basis of today's technology and experience, the waste disposal situation for 2050 would be formidable. From the cumulative total of 1.1 million tonnes, there could be some 400,000 tonnes of spent fuel in temporary storage on perhaps 600-700 sites in 40-50 countries. Some ten depositories would already be full and possibly at least five more scattered strategically throughout the world would be receiving the HLW from the reactor and reprocessing sites. The industry would thus have the task of finding a new site for a HLW store every few years, or, if countries were to refuse to take in others' waste, most countries with nuclear power plants would have to ensure their own storage. This would indeed be a monumental task, if the safety standard of all is to be kept at the required high level.

(c) Reprocessing
Would this option lead to a large expansion of reprocessing? Even though there is considerable controversy about the economics of reprocessing in existing plant, with some arguing for[8] and others against,[9] there appears to be general agreement[10] that under today's conditions of low uranium price and in the absence of FBRs, there is no economic case for building new reprocessing plants. The Japanese plant, presently the only new one being built, is justified as part of the country's long-term energy strategy and in the belief that by the time it is in operation it will have an economic basis.[11,12] Under present plans, reprocessing capacity might by 2020 have reached some 4500 t/yr of heavy metal and might have dealt with 80-100,000 tonnes of spent fuel.

[8] A. Neuberger, *An Economic Evaluation of Thorp*, London Business School, London, October 1993.
[9] F. Berkhout and W. Walker, *THORP and the Economics of Reprocessing*, SPRU, Sussex University, November 1990.
[10] Neuberger, *An Economic Evaluation of Thorp*, op. cit.
[11] Ministry of Foreign Affairs, 'Plutonium, A Renewable Source of Energy: Japan's Policy for Use and Plan for Transport of Plutonium', Tokyo, November 1992.
[12] A. Suzuki, 'Burning up Actinides and Long-lived Fission Products', in M. Grubb, R. Garwin and E. Matanle (eds), *Managing the Plutonium Surplus: Applications and Technical Options*, NATO/Kluwer, forthcoming 1994.

Because commercially proven FBRs are unlikely to be in operation for quite some time, the only commercial use for plutonium from reprocessing is in MOX fuel. This is another subject of heated discord regarding its economic viability under present circumstances, with various US and UK sources arguing one way and French, Belgian and Japanese sources arguing the other. Even if MOX use expands, there should be ample plutonium available from the surplus now building up from civil reprocessing and from the dismantling of nuclear weapons[13] to fuel FBRs as well if or when they come into operation. It is therefore unlikely that economic pressures for more reprocessing facilities will build up until 20 or 30 years into the next century; and even then, as indicated above, the level of incentive will be very dependent on how the uranium resource is viewed at that time. This case assumes that by mid-century nuclear energy will have become an important source of electric power, and the anticipated further growth in electricity demand may well bring to the fore the advantages of making far better use of natural uranium once or if FBRs become commercially accepted.

An argument advanced for considering reprocessing even under today's conditions is that it would reduce the volume of high-level waste and therefore make final disposal easier and cheaper. Others argue, however, that what matters is the radioactivity of the HLW, not the volume, and that the presently used Purex process does not ease the waste problem. This process separates the fission products into different streams, all of which have to be safely disposed of, thereby markedly increasing the total volume of waste (treatment of 1 tonne of spent fuel generates some 14m³ of various grades of waste). Some of these streams are in gaseous form which can only be discharged by venting to the atmosphere, a method that is likely to come under attack as the environmental consciousness of the public increases.[14]

Each of the two most recent plants in France and the UK have a capacity of 800 t HM/yr. Because of the need to minimize radioactive discharges and achieve a very high level of safety, the cost of such plants is high, with figures

---

[13] Albright et al., *World Inventory of Plutonium and Highly Enriched Uranium, 1992*, op. cit., Chapter 5.
[14] W. Häfele, 'The situation at the back end of the fuel cycle', personal communication, March 1991.

of $4.5 billion being quoted for THORP.[15] If and when reprocessing expands, many such plants would have to be built (some twenty even if only 50% of spent fuel were reprocessed by 2050), and there would be a vast increase in the amount of nuclear waste. Hopefully, therefore, technology will have advanced by then, enabling larger and cheaper plants which would produce less waste.

Reprocessing would make the logistics of moving nuclear material around the world even more complicated, especially as it is likely to entail many shipments of plutonium in forms considered by the IAEA to require safeguards.

Summary
In summary, then, Case 3 would in the initial years be no more than a measured expansion of nuclear energy, with no economic pressure for additional reprocessing facilities or for a rush programme to commercialize FBRs. Of course, all the unresolved problems of today, especially provision of waste disposal sites, will need resolution. Beyond 2020, the pace of expansion would accelerate and with that could come the need by mid-century for FBRs and even the possibility of rapid expansion in FBR and reprocessing capacity during the second half of the century. But how realistic is this case?

7.4 Feasibility and public acceptability

Perhaps the first question to resolve is whether, and if so why, anyone would invest in such a major expansion of nuclear energy, bearing in mind the conclusion reached in Chapter 5, that the future of nuclear energy is in the hands of governments. One answer is that specific conditions sometimes apply, as in the case of Japan. But, on the basis of today's knowledge, the only rationale for global expansion is the need to reduce CO_2 emissions, so that governments around the world will ensure that nuclear power stations and all the necessary accompanying infrastructure get built. If, during this period, the present thrust for pro-market policies continues, it has further to be assumed that governments or the international community will have found ways to

---

[15] Neuberger, *An Economic Evaluation of Thorp*, op. cit.

shape the forces in the electricity market in order to achieve the desired results. Whether governments will be able to do this depends on public acceptability: here there appears to be broad agreement that major expansion of
nuclear energy will hinge on its acceptability. As a recent World Energy Council
Report states:[16] '... But, above all, [what really matters is] whether public
concern with operational safety and hazards of waste disposal can be satisfactorily resolved.'

Thus the prime obstacle to major global expansion of nuclear power is the
need for explicit government backing combined with the popular distrust of
this energy form. The public (or at least the opinion-forming part of it) will
need to be satisfied about three frequently expressed worries:

* nuclear accidents with escape of radioactivity
* pollution of the environment by long-life radioactive substances with possible long-term effects on the life-cycle
* nuclear terrorism and proliferation of nuclear weapons.

Such concerns raise the following more specific questions, which are discussed below:

(a) Are nuclear reactors safe enough to make a major accident with signifi-
    cant radioactive release virtually impossible?
(b) Will reprocessing plants be sufficiently safe, especially if they become
    routine in more countries?
(c) Can the handling and permanent disposal of all nuclear waste be made
    sufficiently secure not to endanger future generations?
(d) Will possession of reactors by more countries, plus increased reprocess-
    ing and recycling of plutonium, lead to weapons proliferation and a greater
    likelihood of nuclear terrorism?

There always has to be a compromise between cost and convenience on one
side and safety and security on the other; absolute safety is impossible to
achieve. The public, when asked, obviously calls for the highest possible

---

[16] WEC Commission, *Energy for Tomorrow's World*, op. cit., Chapter 3.

level of safety, but when the bills for all the safety provisions fall due, the same public may well refuse to pay. Where to set the necessary compromise is a matter of political judgment. That is a difficult enough matter when dealing with a project in one's own country, where one can take into account the competence and effectiveness of the people likely to work on the scheme. When it comes to global nuclear questions, one is looking at possible operations in areas with little experience of complex technology, in other regions which may be, or may become, politically unstable, and also at organizations on the fringe of the nuclear contracting industry that are willing to use any method to make a deal.

So as to simplify the situation, some advocates of nuclear energy have suggested that the energy form is more suited to the industrialized world and should not be offered to many of the countries of the developing world. This is, at least for the longer term, quite unrealistic and could not be implemented. Countries now seen to be in one category will move to the other – and it may not just be a one-way movement. Who will judge a country's status? Recent history has taught us that a highly stable and technologically sophisticated country can quickly lose its stability. Given that long term demand growth will be dominated by the developing world, such a restriction would anyway relegate nuclear power to a minor role. Nuclear energy has to be safe enough for most of the world, and seen to be so; if that is not possible, there must be doubts about the acceptability of Case 3.

(a) Reactor safety

As already mentioned in 5.3 above, present design standards for LWRs are set to achieve a chance of one serious accident per 1 million reactor years, assuming US standards of control and supervision (or the UK or French standards, or perhaps those of another handful of countries). Once there are well over 1,000 reactors in perhaps over 50 countries, even such a high safety factor may no longer be adequate and there are views[17] that before entering such an expansion, the design safety standard should be increased by another factor of 10. However, there are indications that improving reactor safety by

---

[17] Häfele, 'Energy from Nuclear Power', op. cit.

adding more and more safety systems can be counter-productive. It increases complexity and cost, without necessarily restoring the confidence of the public, which finds manipulation of such small probabilities difficult to credit. In addition, placing reliance mainly on engineering design to prevent accidents can never be tested and it is therefore impossible to demonstrate that reactors are acceptably safe.[18] Instead, a number of countries – Germany, Sweden, the UK, and especially the US – have devoted their efforts to developing 'inherently safe', perhaps better named 'passively stable' reactors where integrity is maintained without needing the intervention of either operators or automatically operated safety systems, such as secondary cooling pumps or safety valves. The ultimate aim is to produce a design whose safety is sufficiently transparent to 'be understandable, if not to the public, then to the sceptical elite who greatly influence the public's perception of risk'.[19] Because the design should be simpler, it is also hoped that it could be cheaper and suitable for smaller units.

The US Department of Energy is sponsoring work on a number of such designs and the aim was to have some of the first commercial prototypes in operation by the year 2000.[20] However, so far, no funding for such prototypes seems to have been found and it may well be 15 to 20 years before more acceptable reactors of this type become commercially available. In the context of the longer-term future of nuclear power, such a delay is by no means serious, as long as one of the prime purposes of this work is to find designs which are suitable for a major worldwide and publicly acceptable expansion of nuclear energy. The alternative of just sticking to incremental developments of the present LWR designs, on the grounds that they are safe and proven, may well not achieve that aim,[21] however true the nuclear industry may believe this to be.

The answer to this question is, therefore, that adequate reactor safety for a worldwide spread of reactors is possible, but it will need more effort, funds

[18] J.G. Morone and E.J. Woodhouse, *The Demise of Nuclear Energy? Lessons for Democratic Control of Technology*, Yale University Press, New Haven, CT, 1989, Chapters 3 and 4.
[19] C.W. Forsberg and A.M. Weinberg, 'Advanced Reactors, Passive Safety and Acceptance of Nuclear Energy', *Annual Review of Energy*, 1990, Annual Reviews Inc, p. 133.
[20] US National Energy Study, 'Powerful Ideas for America', 1st edition, 1991/2, US Government Publication, 1991, p. 108ff.
[21] D.E. Lilienthal, *Atomic Energy: A New Start*, Harper and Row, 1980.

and time to deliver. Of these, time should be no problem, as in practice the world still has the flexibility to delay a decision on a major nuclear expansion for a few decades yet, with a possible impact on the climate if renewables were to be delayed as well.

(b) Safety of reprocessing plants

Such plants are complex, largely because radioactive materials in solid, liquid and gaseous form are handled throughout the process, which means that a very high standard of containment is necessary to ensure *no* escape of the more dangerous radioactive isotopes present in the spent fuel. This requires a very high level of design, construction and management, though possibly no more so than for some of the more difficult and dangerous chemical plants.

As already mentioned, the present generation of plants is costly and produces large quantities of low- and intermediate-level waste. Even though there is considerable R&D under way, there are views[22] that this process, originally developed to produce near-pure plutonium for the weapons programme, could be radically altered, simplified and made safer if it were tailored more directly to the civil use of plutonium. It should also thereby be possible to reduce the amount of LLW and ILW produced. The cost of such work could be in the region of $2-3 billion, if prototype demonstration units are included, and take 10 to 20 years before a proven and safe process might become available. As there seems little need for more reprocessing plants for quite some while, there should be ample time for this to happen. Unfortunately, there are currently no sponsors for such work, but perhaps that will change, if major expansion of reprocessing comes to be seen as a more necessary or desirable option.

As with reactor safety, therefore, adequate safety of such plants may well be possible, but effort, funds and time are needed to achieve this.

(c) Security of nuclear waste disposal

Technically this should cause no difficulties, as long as one can find areas with the right geological conditions, especially for HLW storage sites, and where public resistance is not too strong. Politically, though, the choice of

---

[22] Häfele, 'The situation at the back end of the fuel cycle', op. cit.

appropriate sites is turning out to be a nightmare. High-level waste sites have to be secure for longer than human history; this raises a number of moral and ethical issues, as well as the need to make absolutely certain that no mistake is made in choosing appropriate sites. This is one reason why the technical investigations of possible sites are taking so long.

As already mentioned in Chapter 2, intermediate-level waste is looked at differently in different countries, but some, such as fuel cladding, may have to join HLW in deep depositories.

Low-level storage sites are less of a problem, but even these have to be kept secure for a few hundred years. Although there are good indications that many suitable sites for such a purpose can be found, strong local opposition is likely to rule a considerable number of them out. Unless there is strong international cooperation and supervision, there would be the danger of inappropriate sites being developed, perhaps in areas where politicians are more 'pliable' and possibly by rogue operators (as has happened in the case of toxic chemical waste). At present there is no international organization responsible for supervision or control, even though the IAEA has issued guidelines for safe repositories.

Here, then, we have a situation where the necessary political and international institutions to ensure safe disposal of nuclear waste do not exist. Without them, the chances of accidents or radioactive pollution must be significant, especially once major expansion of nuclear power has taken place.

(d) The likelihood of proliferation and nuclear terrorism
Up to the present time, countries wishing to achieve nuclear weapons capability focused on the traditional route of uranium enrichment to acquire weapons-grade U-235, and there was little or no connection between these endeavours and power programmes. The question has to be asked, though, whether this pattern will hold in a future in which nuclear power generation would be widespread. Here there are two cases to be examined – the situation without and with reprocessing.

No reprocessing   If a country just imports fresh fuel elements and exports spent fuel for storage elsewhere, a direct connection between nuclear power generation and proliferation is unlikely. Admittedly, 3% enriched uranium in fresh fuel makes enrichment to weapons-grade material that much easier, but as long as all nuclear facilities are under IAEA inspection, which would keep track of fuel elements, clandestine diversion is unlikely. In addition, the enrichment step, even from low enriched feed, would take time and a substantial effort. The route is therefore an improbable one, especially for terrorists.

Another source, at least in theory, would be spent fuel, which contains some 1% plutonium; one year's output from a 1 GW reactor might contain some 200 kg of plutonium. Here, however, the very high radioactivity shields the fuel elements so that covert diversion and reprocessing to separate the plutonium would be very difficult. Considerable research work would be needed, special facilities would have to be set up and the effort involved might be sufficiently large and time-consuming to make detection likely. Nevertheless, such dangers are being treated seriously by the international community, especially by the US and IAEA, and there is talk[23] that measures against proliferation may have to take priority over the transfer of nuclear technology to some states.

Reprocessing   Reprocessing and recycling of plutonium changes the issue. Plutonium from civilian reprocessing can be a direct source for a nuclear explosive, needing only the right expertise.[24] As present intentions are to ship plutonium from reprocessing plants back to their countries of origin, and as over time this will result in stocks of plutonium in an increasing number of countries, terrorists would need to divert only a few tens of kilogrammes of such material to be in business. An alternative to shipping plutonium is to manufacture MOX fuel on reprocessing sites, as is being planned in France and the UK, but, as recently stated by the Deputy Director General of the IAEA, 'Plutonium in mixed oxide form does not present major obstacles to proliferators who wish to isolate the plutonium and return it to weapons use'.[25]

---

[23] J. Simpson, 'A Positive Outlook for Non-proliferation', *ATOM*, January/February 1993, p. 44.
[24] J. Carson Mark, 'Explosive Properties of Reactor-grade Plutonium', *Science and Global Security*, Vol. 4, 1993, p. 111.
[25] W.J. Dircks, 'Non-proliferation Challenges in the Post Cold War World', IAEA, Vienna, Address to the Royal Institute of International Affairs, London, 4 November 1992.

Because of such dangers, suggestions have been made that the IAEA should be asked to provide safeguards for the storage and movement of all plutonium and MOX. According to international usage, *safeguards* are measures designed to detect diversion of materials, so enabling a timely response to be made; the process of guarding designed to prevent theft or damage is called *security*. For facilities under IAEA 'control' the former task is part of that control, but the latter remains in the hands of national authorities or of the owners. Although this may be a possible course of action when only a few countries and a few stockpiles are involved, the proposal becomes quite unmanageable when a major expansion, as is assumed for Case 3, might involve a vast network of plutonium and MOX movement and trade.

Indeed, the present situation is already difficult, with possibly well over 100 tonnes of plutonium from civil reprocessing in stock by the year 2000. Since a similar quantity will become available from the nuclear weapons reduction programmes in Russia and the US, there is considerable concern about how to keep this material safeguarded until it can be utilized or disposed of, and international cooperative efforts are being suggested.[26] Perhaps the early establishment of one or more International Monitored Retrievable Storage (IMRS) sites under IAEA surveillance or even direct UN control might buy time to consider longer-term solutions.[27] In any case, successful resolution of this issue is surely essential for the future of nuclear energy. Considering the public's concerns about nuclear power, any incident of misappropriation of plutonium would strike a major blow against the public acceptability of nuclear energy from which it would take a long time, if ever, to recover.

The answer to the question about proliferation is clear: a major expansion of nuclear power is ultimately – after some decades – likely to lead to reprocessing and plutonium recycling and *if* one assumes today's technology and no stronger international regulatory authorities than are currently available, the chances of proliferation and especially of nuclear terrorism would increase. Yet, with no FBRs for many years, no final HLW storage and an over-supply of uranium, there should be no need to enter the 'plutonium economy' for a

---

[26] Y. Nakasone and A.B. Carter, 'Joint Policy Proposal: Post Cold-War Cooperative Denuclearisation and Plutonium Issues', International Institute for Global Peace, Tokyo and Centre for Science and International Affairs, Harvard University.
[27] Häfele, 'On the Nature of Nuclear Power and its Future', op. cit.

number of decades; meanwhile the dilemma could well be overcome by developments in technology and in building international institutions, such as an international plutonium management system, presently under debate. But there has to be the will to make this happen.

7.5 Conclusions

There has to be doubt whether, on the basis of today's knowledge and conditions, a major worldwide expansion of nuclear energy would be sufficiently safe to achieve public acceptability. Even though continuing and politically accepted developments in a few countries are quite foreseeable, problems start mounting up the more countries get involved. This does not imply that solutions cannot be found, but for the present they are not available. Under such circumstances, deciding to move to major expansion now can be likened to a full passenger plane taking off with the pilot hoping to learn during the flight how to land it.

In summary, of the three cases looked at in this chapter, two are unsatisfactory. Case 1, phasing out, still means resolving the issues of waste disposal and safely running down the nuclear industry over a period of many years; it would also reduce the world's flexibility to ensure provision of adequate energy for the future, especially if the greenhouse effect becomes a serious issue for humanity. On the other hand we do not appear to be ready for the major expansion postulated in Case 3. We are left with Case 2: to continue rather as today, keeping the nuclear option open and so gaining time to find ways of resolving the issues identified in this chapter for the achievement of successful expansion or phase-out.

What that might entail is looked at in the next chapter.

Nuclear II – Another Option?

As has already been argued in previous chapters, under the presently evolving market structures in the electricity industry, private industry is likely to shy away from the nuclear option because of the cost, scale, inflexibilities and time-lags, which all lead to increased financial risks, unless these risks are somehow shared with a supportive government.

Over the past few years a number of voices – many from within the nuclear 'establishment' – have argued that nuclear power, as developed up to now, has become politically unacceptable in a number of countries, but especially in the US, and that it may well not have a future unless the industry accepts that this is happening and finds ways of reversing this trend.[1] According to this view, nuclear power is presently unattractive to private investors for all the reasons described in the previous pages. But it is also argued that the latest technological developments, together with the experience of nuclear energy over the past fifty years, may now make it possible to develop a more benign, acceptable and viable nuclear power industry. Such critics also maintain that any future development should give initial priority to safety and public acceptability rather than to economics. Only once these first aims are achieved should development concentrate on getting the economics right.

There are now also the emerging differences in view between the US and countries such as France, Japan, the UK and Russia about reprocessing and recycling of plutonium and the question of how best to deal with the nuclear materials and waste arising from nuclear disarmament. All this leads to the need for a fundamental review of nuclear strategy which would also take into account some new technological possibilities.

---

[1] (a) J.G. Morone and E.J. Woodhouse, *The Demise of Nuclear Energy? Lessons for Democratic Control of Technology*, Yale University Press, New Haven, CT, 1989, Chapters 3 and 4. (b) A. Weinberg, 'Revisiting the Second Nuclear Era: Probabilities and Practicalities', *Nuclear Engineering International*, November 1992, p. 36. (c) W. Häfele, 'On the Nature of Nuclear Power and its Future', Rossendorf Research Centre, Dresden. Paper given to Global 93 Conference, Seattle, US, September 1993.

8.1 The new technological possibilities

(a) The fuel cycle

Throughout the past ten years two issues have become more and more clear:

(1) The perception of the 1970s about the urgent need for fast breeder reactors to ensure adequate nuclear fuel for a rapid expansion of nuclear energy is outdated, and with it the requirement for reprocessing spent fuel from thermal reactors to provide plutonium for the first FBRs. The difficulty in developing a commercially viable FBR and the supply of plutonium from the weapons programmes means that there is now more than adequate plutonium available for these first-generation FBRs, should they ever be built.

(2) Disposal of nuclear waste is far more difficult than originally envisaged. Whether the reasons are political rather than technological, as the industry tends to argue, or more the realization of possible technological problems, as opponents believe, the issue has to be faced and a solution found.

Laboratories in Russia, France, the US and Japan saw that it might be possible to resolve, or at least ease, the waste problem by modifying the purpose of fast reactors from breeding plutonium to destroying ('burning up') transuranic elements. The principle behind this idea is the fact that most of the fission products in spent fuel from thermal reactors can be fissioned by fast neutrons and converted into less long-lived and less dangerous substances. Such a fission process would generate heat and therefore power, so that the energy content of the fission products (which, of course, include plutonium) need not be lost.

As it was also found in both Russia and France that fast reactors, with the core redesigned and termed Fast Neutron Reactors (FNRs), may well be easier to operate than breeders, the concept of a new nuclear fuel cycle with much reduced nuclear waste production started to look like an achievable goal. There would still be the need to reprocess, but it is claimed that by combining design of the total cycle of fuel fabrication, reprocessing and fast burner, and by having the right ratio between burners and thermal power reactors, it would be possible to stabilize the world plutonium stock and ensure that it would not cause proliferation dangers. As part of such work, the reprocessing step will need to be carefully examined to ensure that it can become part of an acceptable back-end regime for the fuel cycle.

Work on further development of FNR burners includes the use in Russia of molten lead as coolant instead of sodium; in the US the combination of a fast reactor with an electrochemical reprocessing step, making it possible to recycle plutonium and other fission products without leaving the site;[2] and, also in the US, use of linear accelerators to augment the neutron densities in a fast burner.[3] The claims made for such processes are dramatic: that they can generate nuclear power from a range of different materials, including plutonium and transuranic waste products (thereby destroying these problematic materials); and that they can do this with no production of separated plutonium and an output of waste which is both much less in volume and of much shorter radioactive lifetime than that produced by conventional nuclear processes.

The countries mentioned are spending much effort and funds on actively studying these ideas. France hopes to use its two FBR prototypes, Phenix and Superphenix, for large-scale experiments[4] in 'burning' long-lived fission products. Japan is working on a timetable stretching well into the next decade to develop a fast neutron reactor cycle.[5] In the US, a pilot-scale demonstration plant of the combined FNR/reprocessing scheme is nearing completion.

(b) Thermal reactors

This subject was already mentioned in Section 7.4. Although a number of design studies have been made, there has been little practical progress in testing new 'inherently safe' reactors because there is disagreement about whether such a radical departure from the LWR is really necessary. On the

---

[2] C.E. Till, 'Energy over the Centuries: The IFR Option', M. Grubb, R. Garwin and E. Matanle (eds), *Managing the Plutonium Surplus: Applications and Technical Options*, NATO/Kluwer, forthcoming 1994.

[3] C. Bowman, 'Burning up Actinides and Long-lived Fission Products', in Grubb et al. (eds), *Managing the Plutonium Surplus: Applications and Technical Options*, op. cit.

[4] A. MacLachlan, 'Superphenix backed as Actinide Burner', *Nucleonics Week*, 7 January 1993, p. 1.

[5] A. Suzuki, 'Burning Actinides and Long-lived Fission Products', in Grubb et al. (eds), *Managing the Plutonium Surplus*, op. cit.

one side are those who argue that engineered safety is insufficient[6] for public acceptance and that to ensure safety, reactors have become too complex and expensive; on the other side, the industry argues that it would be better to concentrate effort on improvement of existing LWR reactor technology than to spend money and effort on developing other, as yet unproven systems.[7]

A study in the early 1980s by the (American) Institute for Energy Analysis[8] considered this question and found that progress with the LWR has been sufficiently impressive that for US conditions of operation and assuming a minimal threat of terrorism, there is, from the safety point of view, no need to look for substitutes. However, it was also concluded that in the long term and considering the possibility of worldwide extension of nuclear power, it makes sense to have a 'forgiving' reactor available which would cause no danger when faced with poor operation, a low standard of maintenance or sabotage. They found some possible candidates, especially the 'PIUS' reactor from Sweden, which, however, had not reached the stage of detailed design. To take such a project further would require more detailed design studies, followed by economic comparison with other candidates as well as with types already on the market. If it remained satisfactory, a demonstration plant would have to be built to prove the design. Only then would it be possible to offer the design to potential customers. All that might take some 8-10 years.

In the light of that study, it is not surprising that in 1993 in the US a National Research Council committee recommended that it would be better to concentrate on the improvement of existing LWR technology. For good reasons, utilities are never keen to try out new processes. They have had long experience with the present types of reactor and feel that they can judge the risk of installing one. Unless they can be convinced that a new model is better, or that there are severe problems with the present model, they are unlikely to be interested. As the new model is not even developed, there are no data available to convince them of its advantages. To them there is a great deal of sense in the saying 'Better the devil you know than the devil you don't'.

[6] See for example, M. Granger Morgan, 'What Would it Take to Revitalise Nuclear Power in the US?', *Environment*, March 1993, p. 7. See also Chapter 8, note 1 (a) and (b).
[7] B. Wolfe, 'Overview, Nuclear Energy', *Environment*, March 1993, p. 2.
[8] A.M. Weinberg et al., *The Second Nuclear Era. A New Start for Nuclear Power*, Praeger Publishers, 1985.

The US nuclear process industry will be even more committed to the present technology, on which they have spent a great deal of effort and funds. A new type of reactor, which may be smaller, safer and simpler, may be necessary for a worldwide expansion of nuclear power, but there are no guarantees that such an expansion will happen or when. Unless the necessary development work is strongly supported with funds from other sources, such as government, it is difficult to see why process engineering contractors or utilities should take the substantial risk of developing fundamentally new reactors.

8.2 International institutions

In addition to the right technology, a large-scale and widely distributed nuclear industry would need some international organizations to make certain that the high standards required for safe operation were maintained. Even though most countries are likely to have their own safety standards and regulations, the international dimension is necessary, because, as the evidence from Chernobyl demonstrates, the effect of any mishap could cross many frontiers and because the dangers of proliferation and terrorism recognize no frontier.

At present, the IAEA is the only international organization which is officially recognised worldwide. Its main purposes are:

- promotion of nuclear energy by providing technical assistance in the use of this energy form for peaceful purposes
- inspection to detect diversion or misuse of nuclear materials or facilities as part of the Non-proliferation Treaty regime
- provision of advice and guidance on nuclear safety.

The powers of the organization, given to it by the UN Security Council, are strictly circumscribed. It can advise and warn, but cannot control or act, and it can only inspect in countries which have acceded to the Non-proliferation Treaty, and then only those facilities of a country for which it has government permission. In practice, it can be more influential than these constraints imply as long as its warnings are backed by the Security Council, which can act by applying political pressure. The recent case of North Korea may be an example of this.

When contemplating the possibility of large-scale and worldwide use of nuclear energy, the question arises as to whether other international activities, such as the following, may be necessary:

- *Control of safety standards* All the larger countries with nuclear capacity have a Nuclear Inspectorate which has to approve standards and the quality of management and operation, and has to give permission for new plant or procedures to commence. However, with many more countries in play, who will check the quality of the inspectors' work and influence? There have already been international disputes over the siting and safety of nuclear facilities, and serious mistrust of a neighbouring country's concern for safety could easily escalate into an international incident or worse.
- *Control of international movements* Whether or not the developments of the FNR cycle will reduce or even eliminate the dangers of proliferation, many reactors on many sites will mean much movement of radioactive cargoes, including a good number as part of international trade. Taking the oil industry as an example, with its many accidents to tankers, can one leave the control of such movements to individual owners or shippers, or will it be necessary to have strict and enforceable controls?
- *Management of stocks under international control* Recent suggestions about the possibility of an international plutonium depository under multinational supervision[9] raise the issue of whether there will be calls for storage sites, depositories or even special plant to be under international supervision. If that implies having virtual operational control, how would such an aim be met?

In addition to these questions, one has to consider whether the IAEA, as now constituted, could carry out its present range of tasks without being overwhelmed. The Agency today carries out some 9,000 inspections per year for safeguard and verification. Should it be decided, as was recently proposed by the US, that safeguard arrangements be extended to most civil nuclear facilities, but especially to all those which produce, handle or store plutonium and

[9] Y. Nakasone and A.B. Carter, 'Joint Policy Proposal: Post Cold-War Cooperative Denuclearisation and Plutonium Issues', International Institute for Global Peace, Tokyo and Centre for Science and International Affairs, Harvard University.

highly enriched uranium, the number of inspections would have to increase to over 30,000.[10] Unless it becomes possible to change the methodology, the verification task could become unmanageable in the case of global nuclear expansion. Thus new institutional developments need to be considered.

8.3 Nuclear II – how realistic?

Success with technical developments, described earlier, plus the establishment of some new strong international institutions and the strengthening of present ones, could overcome many of the problems mentioned in 7.3 and might therefore give the major expansion of nuclear power a far better chance. But will it happen?

Perhaps the most important priority is to find a way of resolving the issues of proliferation and nuclear waste. As mentioned 8.1a, there seem to be a number of paths which could provide technical resolution by avoiding or greatly reducing the generation of free plutonium, and by destroying the transuranic elements which cause the greatest difficulty for waste disposal. Even allowing for the usual optimism of researchers about their work, it ought to be possible to find at least one route to a solution. At least ten and possibly up to thirty years will be needed, as well as some tens of billions of dollars, before commercially usable designs are available. From the analysis in Chapter 6, it appears that we have the time, though just possibly at the expense of some unwelcome increase in climate change. Availability of funds is a far greater problem.

If this were a matter involving future energy availability and flexibility only, there would be grave doubt as to whether the funds would be forthcoming, given the present economic climate. It would be argued that energy should be a matter of market forces and so should most R&D funding. In reality, most of the important breakthroughs in the energy field over the past 60 years – from nuclear energy, underwater technology and coal gasification to gas turbines and their high-temperature blades – were based on defence-related work

---

[10] T.E. Shea, 'On the Estimation of Future IAEA Verification Costs in Relation to the Safeguarding of Pu and HEU from Military Inventories and in Conjunction with a Fissile Material Production Cutoff', in Grubb et al. (eds), *Managing the Plutonium Surplus: Applications and Technical Options*, op. cit.

which was government-funded, and there is no chance that private companies, with shareholders to consider, would or could spend such sums of money on speculative long-term development.

In this case, though, the position may well be more favourable. The development work is not just needed for future energy supplies, but – more urgently – to find ways of dealing better with nuclear waste, including that from military programmes, and to reduce the chances of nuclear terrorism, also a defence matter. In addition, Japan appears to consider this work to be vital if it is to achieve greater energy self-sufficiency, which again has security connotations. Even though defence expenditure is being cut in most countries, the cost of this development would not be excessive when compared with the cost of the Eurofighter project of around $50 billion, well over $100 billion spent on the Star Wars programme and figures of around $300 billion being mentioned as the possible clean-up cost of waste from the military programmes in the US. If it were possible for the countries now working in this area to join forces, the yearly costs would be even less of a burden.

Another argument in favour of governments finding funds for this work is the likelihood that solution of the waste problem would not only make nuclear energy more attractive, but it would also make its abandonment possible without burdening many future generations with our failures. It just might, therefore, be acceptable to both the pro- and anti-nuclear lobbies.

The case for expenditure on new types of thermal reactors is less clear, but at this stage also less vital. Governments in a number of countries will continue to ensure investment in LWRs. New types of 'inherently safe' reactors will find large-scale use only if nuclear energy becomes a major energy source; that should depend on the success of the work on the FNR cycle, which is likely to have a longer lead time. Flexibility can therefore be retained by delaying significant expenditure on other new reactor development projects until we have a better idea of the nuclear future. At that time, the importance of developing a 'forgiving' reactor, as compared with improvements to the LWR, can be reassessed.

Lastly, there is the question of international institutions. Some of the issues, such as the expanded role of the IAEA or the concept of international plutonium storage, are of immediate relevance and have to be tackled as such. The experience gained can be used in considering the need for other institutions, but little can be done at this stage, except debate and analysis, until we are far clearer what may be necessary and when. It is, however, important not to forget that different futures in terms of nuclear energy could bring different institutional needs. Such needs should, therefore, be part of the nuclear debate.

In summary, then, Nuclear II could well be a technical possibility and there are strong reasons why funds for the most important part of the development – the fuel cycle – should be found. However, it might take quite a number of years before one could be confident of success.

Conclusion: Where to From Here?

This study has attempted to address three main issues. First, *does the world need the flexibility for nuclear energy to become a major energy resource?* To that the answer is 'yes'. Future electricity demand is highly uncertain, the problem of climate change could constrain the use of fossil fuels and there is, as yet, no assurance that renewable energy by itself could take the strain. The importance of electric power to economic growth is such that progress by the developing world could be hampered by lack (or high costs) of energy for power production owing to competition from the industrial world, and this could easily lead to international discord or even worse. The only response to uncertainty is flexibility and hence the need to keep the nuclear option open.

The second question addressed is: *under what conditions would nuclear energy become accepted as a major energy resource of the future?* The most important condition to be met is to achieve full acceptability by the public, which in turn depends on ensuring that expansion does not increase the risk of proliferation and nuclear terrorism, that nuclear waste can be safely and acceptably disposed of, and that nuclear facilities everywhere are sufficiently safe. Use of present-day technology cannot so far deliver, adequately for global expansion, the first two of these requirements and there is discord about the third.

Thirdly, *under what circumstances would utilities and/or governments choose nuclear power rather than other energy sources for power produc-tion?* Here it was found that recent pressures to make the electricity market more competitive and more open to private enterprise will reduce the likeli-hood of investment in nuclear power. The risks for the private investor in choosing nuclear energy rather than other energy sources are likely to be higher, unless a government underwrites some of the risks as part of its energy policy.

We therefore have a dilemma. We need to keep the flexibility to make use of nuclear power, but large-scale expansion on the basis of today's technology is unlikely to be acceptable. The dilemma is worsened by the finding that withdrawal from nuclear energy, as an alternative to expansion, would be a lengthy and expensive undertaking which would reduce the scale of, but not resolve, the safety and security problems identified for expansion. The two most vital issues are how to deal with the nuclear waste, including that from dismantled plant, and how to dispose of the stocks of plutonium without increasing the possibility of such material being diverted for the purpose of proliferation or terrorism. Solutions to these problems have therefore to be found whether the world chooses expansion or withdrawal. The fact that waste from the military nuclear programme also needs to be dealt with and that the dismantling of nuclear weapons will greatly increase the world stock of plutonium adds to the importance of resolving these issues.

Technological developments during the past decade have shown new ways of improving the safety and security of nuclear fuel cycles, for example by making use of integrated fast reactors (FNR) to destroy plutonium and other long-lived radioactive waste products. These, if successfully developed, could considerably reduce the waste problem and dangers of proliferation. Progress has also been made in achieving better understanding of the criteria necessary for the permanent disposal of high-level waste and in the design of simpler and safer thermal reactors. Furthermore the political conditions have changed, with the end of the Cold War bringing for example serious consideration of proposals for an international convention on ceasing the production of separated fissile materials of potential weapons application.[1]

To bring the new technological possibilities to commercial viability and public acceptability would need substantial development efforts, which might take 20-30 years and cost many billions of dollars. There is little doubt that the time is available for such a programme, but it is most unlikely that under present circumstances funds for such long-term programmes could be found from the commercial sector. Most support will have to come from govern-

---

[1] President Clinton, address to the UN General Assembly, 27 September 1993, and background White House fact sheet. A summary is given in 'Trust and Verify', no.41, Verification Information Technology Centre, London, October 1993.

ments, if not for reasons of energy security, then for reasons of general security, especially to reduce the dangers of nuclear terrorism and the need to dispose of nuclear waste.

Should it not be possible to find funds to develop a nuclear technology which would resolve the issue of nuclear waste and proliferation and be acceptable to public opinion, we would be left in the position of being able to plan neither for expansion nor for a phase out that does not still leave burdens for future generations. The most likely outcome would then be to continue to stumble on half-heartedly, until another accident or a terrorist event led to a complete loss of confidence in this energy form, although even then there would be no clear idea what to do about it. Nuclear power would become a 'dangerous diversion'.

Where to from here? The conclusions lead to two basic questions. One is wider than just the nuclear energy field, but covers the future of energy policy as a whole; it relates to the funding of research, development and demonstration (RD&D). The second points to the need to have a clearer idea of what an acceptable nuclear industry providing a significant proportion of the world's electricity power during the mid-21st century might look like, and whether the latest technological developments could get one there.

Research

The uncertainties of growth in electricity demand over the next fifty years are such that the world needs to have the flexibility to respond by having the option of expanding the nuclear sector and/or the ability to make substantial use of renewable fuels. To enable this to happen will require considerable expenditure of money and effort in both the renewable and the nuclear fields. Against these needs, government investment by member countries of the IEA in energy RD&D appears to be declining, with funding of renewable energy projects falling more than most. On the nuclear side, there are indications that adequate expenditure levels might only be forthcoming if they are seen to be associated with defence or security issues. We thus appear to have the grotesque situation that when it comes to risky long-term RD&D, the more benign the area, the greater the disadvantage compared with defence-related fields. This may be the explanation for the point made earlier (in Chapter 8) that most major developments in the energy field appear to have arisen from defence-related work and it may also explain the rather slow progress with renewable energy.

The effect on the long-term energy situation of such selectivity in the choice of funding development activities could be serious. If the necessary nuclear development cannot be 'smuggled in' as defence-related, it may not happen at all, with the result that we may end up in a few decades' time with a nuclear industry which is unacceptable to the public, a renewables industry which is insufficiently developed and an unstoppable increase in CO_2 emissions.

With both governments and private industry more and more cautious about funding energy development and (especially) demonstration, a closer look at this problem, initially perhaps just to achieve better understanding about its dynamics, could be the first step towards a better understanding of how RD&D priorities in the energy field should be set. This is a matter of considerable importance if, as is probable, funds will continue to be limited. How such an investigation might be undertaken is outside the scope of this study, but its results could be vital to the future of nuclear energy.

The nuclear industry of the future

Far better indications than are available today are needed regarding the future shape of a world-scale nuclear energy industry, contributing, say, more than 25% of global electricity demand and fully accepted by the public, and what development effort is needed to get from here to there.

Present debate of this issue is bedevilled by the gulf existing between the pro- and anti-nuclear lobbies. The official view of the former finds it impossible to accept any argument which throws doubt on the excellence of the present industry, as this could be used as a weapon against it, while the anti lobby considers acceptance that nuclear energy might have a long-term future to be an impossible climb-down. Yet both parties must know that the issues are not black or white. On the one side, public acceptance is unlikely to be gained by ignoring criticism and just following Voltaire's Dr Pangloss in announcing that 'All is for the best in the best of all possible worlds'. The other, surely, has to accept that by abolishing nuclear energy tomorrow, one cannot un-invent it and forget all about the problems of waste, spent fuel and the concomitant dangers of nuclear terrorism. Acting like the proverbial ostrich may be good for the ego but not for the environment.

To make progress under such circumstances may need a forum where most interested parties can be represented, so that representatives from the developing and industrial world, from the scientific and defence communities, from politics, business and academic groups and from international organizations can add their wider views to those of the 'experts' from both the industry and its opposition. The prime purpose of such a study would be to try to find an acceptable solution to the problems besetting the future of the nuclear industry and to build a consensus around it. Without such consensus, action is unlikely to follow, however excellent the plan.

The aim of such a forum should be to look for feasible solutions to the technical, economic, security and political problems of nuclear energy, and to consider how they might be achieved. The focus should not be on the short term – next year's investment programme – but in the first instance on what a successful international nuclear industry might look like in 30 or 40 years' time. If such a picture could be agreed on, the next step would be to outline the steps necessary to get there.

More specifically, such a study might address the following issues:

(1) Bearing in mind present research in a number of countries on fast neutron 'burners', the time should now be right to have a new international cooperative look at different fuel cycles, which, in addition to technology and economics, considers public, international, political and social issues. The last such study was completed in 1980.[2] That analysis remains relevant, but a new effort is now needed in the light of the many subsequent developments in the industry, technology, nuclear politics, and various external factors such as climate change, the liberalization of electricity markets, and the end of the Cold War.

(2) Because various countries are carrying out work with similar aims, though perhaps for different reasons, and because of the high cost of this work,

---

[2] International nuclear fuel cycle evaluation, (INFCE), summary and overview, IAEA, Vienna, February 1980.

there is a need to consider how best to achieve cooperation in the RD&D work, although without too great a weakening of competition once commercial use becomes likely. Too early a choice of a development path loses flexibility and can weed out potential winners, while too late a selection can waste much effort, time and money. The political sensitivity of such studies hardly needs stressing.

(3) Another matter for study would be the types of international organizations needed to back up or monitor a successful industry of the future and how these may be formed.

(4) Taking into account the highly uncertain future of the energy field, we need strategies for nuclear energy which make it possible for decision-makers to choose options during this decade while still being able to react flexibly to future events as these unfold.

It has to be recognized that a number of past major studies of nuclear issues have failed to achieve their purpose by either failing to reach conclusions or ending up being ignored. Studies in other areas, such as the climate change work (through the Intergovernmental Panel on Climate Change) and the ozone layer investigation, have been highly influential. Because nuclear energy is such a controversial subject and because a solution regarding nuclear waste *has* to be found whatever the future of the energy form, it is surely worthwhile making such an attempt with this subject.

Recent political changes, such as the end of the Cold War, the disintegration of the USSR, and especially the effect of nuclear disarmament have shown the need for a new look at the connection between the future development of nuclear energy and the future of the non-proliferation regime. The two fields already interlink within the IAEA, and the future of the Non-proliferation Treaty (NPT) and the regime developed from it is due for a fundamental reappraisal during 1995. The NPT Extension/Review Conference could therefore be an excellent opportunity for launching such an international programme of assessment and consensus-building.

Should such a forum reach no agreement or find no path to a successful nuclear future, we would at least know which issues cannot be resolved, and the international energy community would have a better concept of how far nuclear energy can be trusted to take up future energy demand. Many of the issues identified in this study were already considered in the Acheson-Lilienthal Report of 1946 and by President Ford and a number of others in the 1970s, but they remain unresolved. Meanwhile the problems of security are mounting, and plutonium and waste stockpiles are getting larger. With the end of the Cold War, perhaps now the time is right and the will exists to find solutions. The alternative is to admit failure and hand the problem to future generations with the message that we failed; hopefully it will not be too late for them to do better.

Glossary

Actinide: one of the heavy elements actinium, thorium, protactinium, uranium, neptunium, plutonium, americium, curium, berkelium and californium, all of which are chemically very similar; actinides of interest are those which are long half-life alpha-emitters.

Activation: absorption of neutrons to make a substance radioactive

Alpha particle: high-energy helium nucleus (two protons, two neutrons) emitted by some radioactive nuclei.

Beta particle: high-energy electron emitted by radioactive nucleus.

Breeder: reactor which produces more fissile nuclei than it consumes.

Burner: reactor which consumes more fissile nuclei than it produces.

BWR: boiling water reactor.

Cladding: sometimes just Clad (as noun): metal sheath (Magnox, zircalloy, stainless steel or ceramic) within which reactor fuel is hermetically sealed.

Containment: structure within a reactor building – or the building itself – which acts as a barrier to contain any radioactivity which may escape from the reactor.

Control rod: rod of neutron-absorbing material inserted into reactor core to 'soak' up neutrons and shut off or reduce rate of fission reaction.

Coolant: liquid (water, molten metal) or gas (carbon dioxide, helium, air) pumped through reactor core to remove heat generated in the core.

Cooling pond: deep tank of water into which irradiated fuel is stored on removal from a reactor, where it remains until shipped for reprocessing or long-term storage/disposal.

Core: the region of a reactor containing fuel (and moderator, if any) within which the fission reaction is occurring.

Critical: refers to a chain reaction in which the total number of neutrons in one 'generation' of a chain is the same as the total number of neutrons in the next 'generation' of the chain; that is, a system in which the neutron density is neither increasing nor decreasing.

Decay: spontaneous radioactive transformation.

Depleted uranium: uranium with less than the natural proportion (0.7%) of uranium-235, which has been removed in an enrichment process and transferred to the remaining 'enriched' uranium.

Deuterium: hydrogen-2, heavy hydrogen; its nucleus consists of one proton plus one neutron, rather than the one proton only of ordinary hydrogen.

Diversion: euphemism for theft, or the 'improper' appropriation of nuclear material, usually considered as for potential weapons application.

Enriched, as in enriched uranium: uranium in which the proportion of uranium-235 has been increased above the natural 0.7%

Enrichment: process of making enriched uranium.

Fast burner: fast reactor designed to produce fewer fissile nuclei than it consumes.

Fast neutron: high energy neutron, direct from fission.

Fast breeder: reactor designed to have conversion ratio greater than one, using un-moderated fast neutrons.

FBR: fast breeder reactor.

Fertile: material like uranium-238 or thorium-232, which can by neutron absorption be transformed into fissile material.

Fissile: capable of undergoing fission.

Fission: rupture of a nucleus into two lighter fragments (Fission products) plus free neutrons – either spontaneously or as a consequence of absorption of a neutron.

Fuel: material (such as natural or enriched uranium or uranium and/or plutonium dioxide) containing fissile nuclei, fabricated into a suitable form for use in a reactor core.

Fusion: the combination of two light nuclei to form a single heavier nucleus.

Gamma ray: high-energy electromagnetic radiation of great penetrating power emitted by nucleus.

Gigawatt: one thousand million watts.

Graphite: black compacted crystalline carbon, used as neutron moderator and reflector in reactor cores.

ILW: of radioactive waste, intermediate level waste.

Half-life: period of time within which half the nuclei in a sample of radioactive material undergo decay; characteristic constant for Isotope.

Heavy hydrogen: see Deuterium.

Heavy water: Deuterium dioxide – water in which the hydrogen atoms are 'heavy hydrogen' (deuterium).

Helium: light chemically inert gas used as coolant in high temperature reactors.

HLW: of radioactive waste, intensely radioactive with medium to long half-life.

IAEA: International Atomic Energy Agency.

Iodine: as iodine-131; biologically hazardous fission product of short half-life (8 days) which tends to accumulate in the thyroid gland.

Irradiated: of reactor fuel, having been involved in a chain reaction, and having thereby accumulated fission products in any application, exposed to radiation.

Isotope: form of an element, with the same number of protons in its nucleus as all other varieties (isotopes) of the element, but a different number of neutrons.

Krypton: a chemically inert gas; the isotope krypton-85 is a fission product at present released to the atmosphere from reprocessing plants.

LLW: of radioactive waste, not particularly radioactive.

LWR: light water reactor – either pressurized water reactor or boiling water reactor.

McMahon act: The US Atomic Energy Act 1946, which banned any further transfer of nuclear information from the US to the erstwhile allies Britain and Canada, and set up the US Atomic Energy Commission (AEC) and the Joint Congressional Committee on Atomic Energy (JCAE).

Mixed oxide: of reactor fuel, fuel in which the fissile nuclei are plutonium-239, mixed with natural or depleted uranium in a proportion equivalent to enriched uranium.

Moderator: material whose nuclei are predominantly of low atomic weight (e.g. light water, heavy water, graphite) used in reactor core to slow down fast neutrons to increase probability of their absorption in uranium-235 or plutonium-239 to cause fission.

MWe: megawatts electric.

Neutron: uncharged particle, constituent of nucleus – ejected at high energy during fission, capable of being absorbed in another nucleus and bringing about further fission or radioactive behaviour.

NPT: Non-proliferation Treaty, intended to control the spread of nuclear weapons and their technology.

Plutonium: heavy metal, made by neutron bombardment of uranium; fissile, highly reactive chemically, toxic and radioactive (alpha emitter).

Price-Anderson Act: US Act of Congress limiting the third-party insurance liability of reactor operators in the event of an accident, and providing Federal indemnity to this limit.

Purex: plutonium-uranium extraction; original technology for reprocessing of irradiated reactor fuel.

PWR: pressurized water reactor.

Radiation, Nuclear: neutrons, alpha or beta particles or gamma rays which radiate out from radioactive substances.

Radioactivity: behaviour of substance in which nuclei are undergoing transformation and emitting radiation; note that radioactivity produces radiation – the two terms are not equivalent.

Reflector: of neutrons, a material of low atomic weight (light or heavy water, graphite) around a reactor core to reflect neutrons back into the reaction region.

Refuelling: replacement of reactor fuel after it has sustained maximum feasible burn-up; necessitated by loss of reactivity, build-up of neutron-absorbing fission products, and cumulative damage from radiation, temperature, coolant etc.

Reprocessing: mechanical and chemical treatment of irradiated fuel to remove fission products and recover fissile material.

Safeguards: term applied to keeping track of special nuclear material to prevent diversion.

Tailings: fine grey sand, left over from extraction of uranium from ore; it contains radium, emits radon.

Thorium: fertile heavy metal.

Transuranic: those with an atomic number greater than that of uranium (which is 92) and include plutonium and other long-lived fission products.

Tritium: hydrogen-3 – nucleus contains one proton plus two neutrons; radioactive.

Uranium: heaviest natural element, dark grey metal; isotopes 233 and 235 are fissile, 238 is fertile; alpha-emitter.

Uranium hexafluoride, easily vaporized uranium compound used in enrichment processes, also termed 'Hex'.

Yellowcake: mixed uranium oxides, with formula U_3O_8, produced from uranium ore by extraction process in uranium mill.

Source: Adapted (with permission and many thanks) from W.C. Patterson, *Nuclear Power*, (second edition) Pelican, 1983, London.

Other Publications from the
Energy and Environmental Programme

Books

* *The Earth Summit Agreements: A Guide and Assessment*, Michael Grubb et al, April 1993, £12.50 pbk, £25 hbk

Emerging Energy Technologies: Impacts and Policy Implications, Michael Grubb et al, June 1992, £29.50 hbk

The Environment in International Relations, Caroline Thomas, May 1992, £12.50 pbk, £25 hbk

Energy Policies and the Greenhouse Effect Volume One: Policy Appraisal, Michael Grubb, 1990, £12.50 pbk, £29.50 hbk. *Volume Two: Country Studies and Technical Options*, Michael Grubb et al, 1991 £12.50 pbk, £35.00 hbk

European Gas Markets: Challenge and Opportunity in the 1990s, Jonathan P. Stern, 1990, £25 hbk only

Reports and Occasional Papers

* *Power from Plants: The Global Implications of New Technologies for Electricity from Biomass*, Walt Patterson, April 1994, £9.95

The Struggle for Power in Europe: Competition and Regulation in the EC Electricity Industry, Francis McGowan, 1993, £12.50

Evolution of Oil Markets: Trading Instruments and their Role in Oil Price Formation, Joe Roeber, 1993, £12.50

Oil and Gas in the Former Soviet Union: the Changing Foreign Investment Agenda, Jonathan P. Stern, 1993, £9.50

* *Environmental Profiles of European Business*, Dion Vaughan and Craig Mickle, April 1993, £15

Third Party Access in European Gas Industries: Regulation-driven or Market-led? Jonathan P. Stern, November 1992, £12.50

Paradise Deferred: Environmental Policymaking in Central and Eastern Europe, Duncan Fisher, June 1992, £10

Energy and Environmental Conflicts in East/Central Europe: the Case of Power Generation, Jeremy Russell, 1991, £10

Environmental Issues in Eastern Europe: Setting an Agenda, Jeremy Russell, 2nd edition 1991, £10

The Greenhouse Effect: Negotiating Targets, Michael Grubb, 2nd edition 1992, £10

The UK 'Coal Crisis': Origins and Resolutions, Mike Parker, October 1993, £7.50

Climate Change Policy in the European Community: Report of a Workshop, Pier Vellinga and Michael Grubb (eds), April 1993, £7.50

To order the above, and for further information about publications and the Programme's work, contact the Energy and Environmental Programme, Royal Institute of International Affairs, 10 St James's Square, London SW1Y 4LE. Tel: + 44 71-957-5711, Fax: + 44 71-957-5710. Publications marked * are also available from Earthscan Publications Ltd, 120 Pentonville Road, London N1. Tel + 44 71 278 0433, Fax: + 44 71 278 1142.